D0227600

Understanding
Your Pony

Understanding Your Pony

Lucy Rees

Stanley Paul
London Sydney Auckland Johannesburg

By the same author

The Horse's Mind
Keeping a Pony

Stanley Paul & Co. Ltd
An imprint of the Random Century Group
20 Vauxhall Bridge Road, London SW1V 2SA

Random Century Australia (Pty) Ltd
20 Alfred Street, Milsons Point, Sydney, NSW 2061

Random Century New Zealand Limited
191 Archers Road, PO Box 40-086, Glenfield,
Auckland 10

Century Hutchinson South Africa (Pty) Ltd
PO Box 337, Bergvlei 2012, South Africa

First published 1991

Copyright © Lucy Rees 1991

The right of Lucy Rees to be identified as the author
of this work has been asserted by her in accordance
with the Copyright, Designs and Patents Act, 1988

Set in 11/13 pt Times Roman by Input Typesetting Ltd,
London

Printed and bound in Great Britain by Clays Ltd, St. Ives PLC

British Library Cataloguing in Publication Data
Rees, Lucy 1943–
Understanding your pony.
1. Livestock. Ponies
I. Title
636.16

ISBN 0 09 174217 X

Illustrations by Sara Moller

Contents

			Page
Chapter	*1*	Introduction	7
Chapter	*2*	The Wild Ones	15
Chapter	*3*	The mustang in your field	21
Chapter	*4*	Senses	35
Chapter	*5*	Language	53
Chapter	*6*	What you tell your pony	95
Chapter	*7*	What's he like?	107
Chapter	*8*	Bullies, leaders and friends	121
Chapter	*9*	Learning and teaching	133
Chapter	*10*	Coping with obstinacy	147
Chapter	*11*	Worse difficulties	154
Chapter	*12*	Ends and beginnings	169
		Index	174

Chapter 1

Introduction

'He's got a mind of his own,' people say, often sounding rather surprised, about their ponies. Of course ponies have minds of their own. Even when we treat them like motorbikes, polishing them, kicking them and roaring off down the lane on them, they think and feel for themselves.

When you first start to ride and handle ponies, you are often taught as if it were all about arranging your arms and legs in the right way and pushing the right buttons. As you may have found, the buttons don't always work. Ponies get surprised, worried, excited, frightened, miserable and happy just as we do. The trouble is that we're different kinds of animals. We may have the same kinds of feelings, but they're not about the same things.

This book is about the way ponies think and feel, and how to tell what they are feeling. Everybody who has been around horses for a long time learns this by experience, but there are short cuts. For some reason horsepeople haven't spent much time writing down how or why a pony behaves the way he does. I think this is because we are a bit swell-headed about being so much cleverer than they are.

Being clever is only one of the things that brains are for. Although we still don't know exactly how brains work, we do know that different parts of them do different things. There are parts that are to do with keeping your balance and controlling your movements (cerebellum), parts to do with understanding what we see, hear, touch and so on, and parts to do with appetites like being hungry and thirsty. There are also parts that are to do with feelings, with anger, frustration, tenderness and joy: emotions in general (limbic system). These areas are just as big and complicated in horses as they are in us, and it is reasonable to suppose that horses and dogs have just as strong emotions as we do. They certainly behave as if they do.

Other parts (neocortex) are to do with thinking, with understanding why things happen, working out problems, imagining things, and putting all this into words or pictures. These bits aren't very big in horses. In our brains they are enormous. We are better, not just a bit better but amazingly much better, at thinking and imagining than are any other animals. You can think about your feelings, and often do. You can even change your feelings by thinking about them. You can cheer yourself out of depression by thinking of good things to come, talk yourself out of the terrors of a nightmare, or invent ways of not getting upset by someone who is horrid to you.

A pony can't do that. He can't think about his feelings. It's terribly difficult for us to imagine what it would be like not to be able to think about our feelings. To live always in the present, not to be able to imagine the future, not to be able to work out why someone is in a funny mood, not to be able to understand what you are doing wrong or promise to do better next time: it's a strange idea. But that is what life is like for a pony. He likes what he likes, he feels angry, happy, scared, glad to be with his friends without wondering why, or whether he is right, or what he can do about it.

That doesn't mean that ponies can't learn. They have excellent memories, better than ours for some things. Learning isn't necessarily to do with thinking: you probably know the words of all sorts of nonsensical pop songs, without having thought much about them. Learning is to do with repeating things and whether they give you pleasure or pain. A pony can learn not to be afraid, if we push him into something that scares him and he finds it doesn't hurt after all. He learns even better if he finds it brings a reward. But he can't use reason to argue himself out of his fear, as you might.

This is an enormous difference between us and ponies. But it seems to me that being so much cleverer than they are doesn't mean we should say they are stupid and ignore their feelings. What we should do, surely, is to use our cleverness and imagination to work out why they feel the way they do, and to use that understanding to get on better with them.

I have spent a great deal of time watching and thinking about the way animals behave. It's always fascinated me. Partly, I think, it's because when I was a child I couldn't for the life of me work out how I, as a person, was supposed to behave. I seemed to do everything wrong. People and the rules they made baffled me. Animals baffled me less. In the woods and mountains, it seemed, they lived so much more simply, pleasantly and peacefully: no

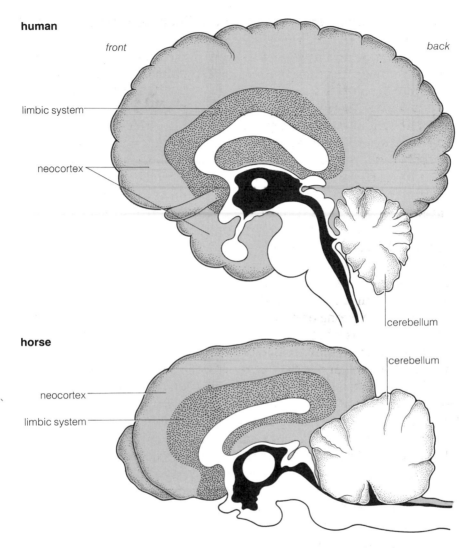

human

front

back

limbic system

neocortex

cerebellum

horse

cerebellum

neocortex

limbic system

Diagrams of your brain and your horse's brain, cut in half. The front is at the left.

The brain is a hollow tube with thick walls. In some places the walls are so thick that they are folded, and may overlap other parts. Here the black part is the hollow. At the back of the brain is the cerebellum, which controls your movements. Your horse's cerebellum is bigger than yours, like his body. Below that is the part that controls your breathing and alertness. The front part of the brain is in overlapping layers. The outside layer (neocortex) seems to deal with thinking, imagining, planning and talking. The inner layer (limbic system) seems to deal with your feelings and emotional reactions, for instance to pain or pleasure. The limbic system is about the same size in both of you. But in your brain the neocortex is huge, mushrooming out over the back and down the sides of the rest of the brain. Your brain is about twice the size of your horse's, and most of the extra is neocortex. The white sausage-shaped bit in the middle is the connection between the right and left sides of the front part of the brain.

laying the table, no lectures about manners, no refrigerators, no bills, no homework, no tears, no being sent to bed for saying the wrong thing or ripping their clothes. I found their ways a lot nicer to think about than those of my family, and their behaviour made a lot more sense.

I studied animal behaviour at university, learned about the rules of learning, and started breaking in young ponies and horses and teaching people to ride them. I'd ridden since I could walk but I'd never had a formal lesson in my life, so I didn't know much about techniques. But I soon found that the more you understand behaviour the less you need to depend on techniques. I had the best teachers of pony behaviour: wild-eyed creatures off the hills who knew nothing about people except that they were best avoided, and at a flat-out gallop. They behaved like foxes or deer, with only their instincts to guide them. I had to learn what these instincts were.

Young horses, and the miserable 'problem' horses I've since dealt with, are all a bit like that. They are raw. Their behaviour, even when it seems crazy and stupid in a stable yard, makes perfect sense for an animal that should be galloping around in a herd on a fenceless mountain. It is often less easy to learn about horse behaviour from older ponies, for we train some of that rawness out, though some of it still remains. The rules, the overall patterns that make sense, are less obvious.

In this book I've put down some of the things that horses have done which have made me think about the rules and patterns of horse sense. You'll see some of them in your own ponies. The pony that I mention most often, because I have known him so long and he has shown me so many things, is Pete. He deserves a proper introduction.

Pete's mother is a nondescript little pony that once escaped, came back a fortnight later with a smug expression, and produced him eleven months later. She must have had good taste, for his unknown father was certainly an Arab. I met Pete when he was ten months old, weaned, gelded, lonely and skinny, a bundle of long lovely legs and a sweet head. He was not what I wanted: too small, underfed, scared . . . but he floated across the hillside like a swallow, scarcely seeming to touch the ground, and even now, at twenty, he still does.

When I'd befriended him, he'd follow me like a dog on long rambles up the mountains, skipping off to poke his nose into anything that interested him and scampering back to hide behind me when he was scared. He'd known only his mother, and that only

Pete enjoys dashing about on mountainsides that make you dizzy to look down.
Here he is playing while out on a walk with me

for five months, so he had to teach himself how to behave while I watched him. He always assumed I understood his expressions, so I had to. (Unfortunately he thinks everybody else does too, and gets annoyed when they seem to ignore him.)

He grew to 14.1, most of it legs. I thought him too small for me to ride seriously, so for several years I'd ride him a bit, let him wander, then ride again. In fact he's very strong in the back, and since then he's carried me the length and breadth of Wales several times over. He's the best of travelling companions, always alert, always sensitive, and he loves nothing better than a good new view.

Perhaps it's because he's had so much more freedom than most ponies that he's a genius. I don't honestly know. He might have been a genius anyway. But he certainly is. It's difficult to say exactly how, and it may be partly because these wild, rugged mountains give more scope for geniuses to reveal themselves, but everybody who has been with him for any length of time has come back, eyes shining, gasping: 'Do you know what Pete's just done?' His wisdom constantly astonishes people. He's not clever in our sense, but he uses his pony-cleverness to its utmost, with amazing results.

Once I was asked if I could take him to the top of Cnicht, the mountain I live on, for a film. It's terribly steep and dangerous, but he'd been most of the way before. A few days before filming we went up to check the way. At the head of the valley you climb steeply, then go up a narrow gully choked with rocks. Tiny streams, bits of bog, and sudden holes between the rocks mean that for half a mile or more you twist, turn and jump about, often with only one possible safe place to put a foot. It's not a place I would dream of taking any other pony except one bred there. Then there's a 45° scree slope, a slide of loose stones, with a sheep path only as wide as a pony's foot going across half-way up it. The scree drops straight into a lake, so you can't afford to slip. Another difficult gully, another steep climb, and you're on the final ridge. It's a desperate place. Wonderful view, though.

That night it snowed, and went on for three days until everything was blanketed in white. The film company phoned to say they'd be coming to film next day from a helicopter. I said it was impossible. But they insisted: they'd paid for the helicopter and crew, it was to be sunny, and so on. Finally I said I would take Pete up the slope at the end of the valley, where there's an old quarry track. The pictures would be pretty and he would be safe. I wasn't going to risk him on the mountain.

But when we floundered up the slope, over my wellies in snow, Pete wouldn't head for the quarry. He kept pulling off towards the

Part of the way that Pete had to go up, when it was covered in snow. He puts his head low to make sure of his footing going through the rocks. If you are riding in a difficult place like this you must let your reins slip through your fingers so the pony can see properly; otherwise he may refuse to go on, or stumble if he does

way up Cnicht and getting annoyed with me. I fell down and let go of him, and he shot off across the slope. By the time I caught up with him he had started up the first gully. It was choked with snow, with just the occasional rock poking its head out. The stream down the middle, the trickles that feed it and all the holes and boggy bits were completely hidden. But Pete was dancing.

He was dancing slowly through the unbroken snow, weaving this way and that, jumping a little here, taking a big step there, changing feet, and thinking. Remembering. When I took a straight line instead of following his steps I tripped over the hidden rocks, fell into the invisible streams, sank into the bogs he'd stepped round. What he was doing was remembering every step of the way without being able to see it, concentrating so hard that he was furious with me every time I disturbed him.

The scree slope was an unbroken sweep of snow, and I thought he must stop. But he started across it confidently and I followed, finding the path under my feet, scarcely daring to breathe until I reached the other side. He did his slow dance up the second gully. Even though it was happening I could barely believe this extraordinary feat of memory. Although he had the occasional clue from a big rock sticking out of the snow, he was remembering his moves as a dancer does, remembering the exact twists, the size of his steps, how one followed another, from just one practice earlier that week. I doubt that even a highly trained dancer could remember a whole three hours' solo performance from one practice, especially if he were not warned he'd have to remember it.

Pete got his reward. The summit ridge was blasted clear of snow and the rough grass sticking through the ice gave enough foothold for us to gallop to the top with the helicopter whirring above us. The top's a scramble but he was determined. I'm sure he must be the only pony to have seen half of Wales covered with snow on a brilliant day. I had a hard job persuading him to come down. He does love a good view.

Again he'd set me thinking. Why was he so determined to get to the top? How had he remembered the way so brilliantly? Why is remembering the way so important? Why does he love to exercise his memory like that? Does he remember everywhere he's been?

To find the answers to these and many other questions that ponies' behaviour makes us ask, we have to look at how wild ponies live. Ponies don't have brilliant memories in order to be in films, or to do dressage tests. Brilliant memories help them stay alive.

Chapter 2

The Wild Ones

Noon. In the warm spring sun a yearling, his winter coat peeling in tatters from him, lies flat on his side, one ear twitching, listening to his mother stamp and scratch at flies close by him. She and her friend, both big with foal, stand nodding under an ancient thorn tree, half asleep. Before them waves of land, speckled with scrubby trees, roll on like the sea towards steep, snow-capped mountains; around them two other mares and some youngsters are dozing with heads low and hips aslant. Only the stallion is alert. Ears pricked, a bunch of grass hanging forgotten from his mouth, he stares at a distant rise, attention caught by a movement far off..

From where the little band of horses is resting you can see for miles: the look-out spot under this huge old tree has been a favourite loafing place for generations of their forerunners, for the breeze wafting up from the lower plains keeps most of the flies away, and nothing can creep up on you unseen. The earth is stamped hard as a board, and the bushes around have been nibbled and stunted; narrow paths lead off in all directions.

The stallion frowns, neck outstretched. Suddenly he raises his head, snaps into a position as taut as a soldier saluting, and snorts softly. The mare nearest him, the oldest of the group and grand-mother to the colt, is instantly alert, copying him; the colt's mother swings round to see the excitement, nickering softly to her son who rolls on to his side. But the old mare, calmer than the stallion, has realised that the distant movements that caught his eye are not lion or wolf but little deer. Harmless. She sighs and goes back to dozing while the stallion, left with a wide-awake feeling and nothing to do with it, switches his attention to one of the mares. He strolls over to her, mouth half-open, nickering; touches her nose; sniffs her head, neck and shoulder, and starts to nibble her; scratches her heartily as she starts to scratch him, and then wanders off to pick at a thorn bush, lips rolled delicately back from his teeth.

Half an hour later the colt rises, stretches with his back leg stuck out and his neck arched, bounces on the spot and springs into bucks and leaps. Trotting over to his friend, a filly of his own age, he prances flirtatiously, inviting her to play. It is a wild romp of racing and bucking that soon attracts the two-year-olds. They are a rude, rough lot, teasing the adults and lungeing at the yearlings in mock attacks. The filly, leaping away, bumps against one of the older mares and gets kicked for her carelessness, so she limps back to her mother for comfort, tail between her legs, jawing soundlessly.

The youngsters' game has woken everybody and they stretch, scratch and blow their noses. The old mare shakes herself and sets off down the path that leads to the big river ten miles away. The others fall into line behind her: first her friend, almost as old; then her daughter and her daughter's friend. Friendships are strong in this small group and the mares always travel in pairs, the old mare

Under their favourite tree, the wild horses relax. The stallion has just spotted something in the distance. The way he is standing, with his tail up, calls attention to himself. But as yet only one foal has noticed him. The two old mares are asleep together; the two younger mares, who are also friends, are scratching each other's withers. The stallion will now snort or move jerkily to make the mares look at what he has seen

first, the youngsters trying to squeeze into line or cavorting about with the stallion snapping at their heels like a sheepdog.

They follow a well-worn track, the old mare marching purposefully down to a hollow of lush spring grass. After eighteen years she knows every tree and stone in this country. She knows the best place to be when the bitter wind comes sweeping down from the mountains or when the heat rises from the plain; she knows where acorns are in autumn and bright beech leaves in spring, where the wild plums grow and which water is best; she knows to go up in summer, when mountain grass is sweeter and flies are fewer, and to come down for winter; she knows the best foaling spots and where marshes form in wet weather.

Every fear or pleasure in this mare's life happened at a particular place and time, and that is how she remembers them. Each spot she passes has its memories, good or bad, according to the season and the weather. Some of this she learned from her mother and some on her own, but it has been passed round and become the knowledge of the group. Never has she led the herd into the little box-canyon where, years ago, this group's parents were trapped and a foal was killed by wolves; possibly, when she is gone and her warnings have faded, some bold youngster will rediscover it and be exposed to the danger again. Often in autumn, a few weeks after a summer flood, she has led them deliberately to a part of the riverbank where they wander about puzzled, for there is nothing special there. What she remembers is a wonderful feast of sweet new grass that sprang up once at the same time, and she is ever hopeful of finding the same again; what she cannot know is that on that occasion a herd of wild pig had grubbed up the earth, leaving a tilth that the edges of the flood reseeded. The grass is never what she remembers; but she hopes and revisits all the same, and no doubt one day she will be rewarded.

This time, though, she is heading for another little meadow in the midst of some trees. To reach it they must pass through a narrow wooded gorge they all dislike. They are alert and afraid, for here a lion could leap off the bank on to an unsuspecting back and there would be nothing to save the victim. They scuttle through quickly, the youngsters huddling close to their mothers, but as they reach the far end a noise on the bank startles them. Instantly they are galloping, heading for the wooded slopes beyond, while the stallion, forgetting about chasing them, tips his head up to look behind him as he goes. Seeing nothing, he finally wheels, stops, snorts and waits. A moment later he hears the grunts: wild pig, digging for roots. They are harmless at this distance, but they're things to stay away from: they sleep so soundly that you can tread on one asleep and break your leg, or have it cut by furious tusks, while mother pigs will attack to defend their babies. He snorts again to drive them away and sets about collecting the mares. Grumpily the old mare leads them further to the open land beyond the woods, where a lion will have to make a dash to reach them.

And here they can eat, and doze, and eat again: a lazy life, though there is plenty of interest in sorting through the herbs and grasses, and they are still thin after the winter. On lush grazing it does not take them long to fill their small stomachs, so they rest and then play before moving on. The mares are staid lumps, seldom bothering to move more than absolutely necessary, but by the evening the colt is so restless that he searches out his filly friend and draws her away from the group. Together they go exploring, excited and scared as children alone at a funfair, spooking at shadows and snorting at stones until they leap for each other's protection so hard they collide. When they retrace their steps they find the mares have gone.

At first they are shocked and stupid, running about neighing shrilly, but when no answer comes they start using their noses. Soon they pick up the trail, but they come across a pile of dung that puzzles them again. Of course it smells of stallion: the stallion leaves his mark on top of anyone else's, to warn off other stallions; but the dung underneath belongs to the colt's mother, and it smells odd. It is certainly hers, but it has a weird tang. The colt breathes it in deeply, bending low to fill each nostril then raising his head and turning back his lip to roll the smell around in the back of his nose. Definitely odd. Neighing again, he dashes along the path the mares have taken, the filly at his heels.

They soon find his mother. She has gone off the path and is standing exhausted in a patch of soft ground. She still smells odd. And she does not want to know her son, kicking him away, panting. The filly wants her own mother, so the colt follows her, though hesitantly. When they find the group the stallion herds them in, snapping and bumping at them half-angrily, half-playfully: he does not mind the older colts leaving the group and indeed will soon drive them away when the mares start to breed again, but this colt is too young. His place is still with the group.

After dark, though, the colt frets for his mother, for the group is on the move again, away from her. He slips away, but he is nervous on his own: torn between his longing to be with his mother, his need for the group, and his fear, he dashes to and fro along the path, calling, stopping, listening, back and forth. It is this that

A bunch of mustangs in Utah. The mares have made off in their usual marching order. The stallion stayed behind to try to scare me away but then hurried after them. In this semi-desert the horses always find something to eat but they are in real danger from rattlesnakes, mountain lion, javelina (wild pigs) or stepping into gopher holes. There are also flash floods, whole rivers that suddenly sweep down from the mountains

nearly leads to disaster, for a family of wolves not far off hear him. Their furry ears prick; they start loping in his direction.

The colt's careering up and down is so senseless that the wolves stop to work out the right moment to strike. He is a strong colt and it will take luck and a well-timed attack to bring him down. They have worked upwind towards him but as he trots away from them he is startled by a rabbit dashing across the path. He stops, turns, gallops past the waiting pack, stops, wheels, neighs and listens. In this brief chance moment, panting, he catches a whiff of wolf on the light night air. It is enough. As they charge he has already shot away, flat out back to the group who, hearing the drumming of his hoofs, are already on their toes. When he dashes into their midst, wild-eyed, wolves not far behind, they are gone in a flurry, bunched tightly together, galloping for their lives. They know every stone and twist on this path and even in the dark do not put a foot wrong. As they come into more open country they are drawing ahead, for though a wolf's plans may catch a lone horse or wear down an unfit one, a close-packed whirlwind of hard-galloping hoofs offers no weak point to attack. The wolves note the strength of the group, the lack of stragglers, the stallion at their heels, and realise this is not their lucky night. When the horses reach a knoll and stop where any attack must be made up an open slope, they can see the wolves trotting below them down to the marshes, for it is frog-mating time and there is easier game to be had there.

Far behind, in her little clearing, the lone mare hears the commotion disappear into the distance and allows her full belly to relax, though it is hours before she feels safe enough to lie down uncomfortably. Twenty minutes later she is nuzzling her fourth foal, another colt, urging him to be on his feet and away from this place where the smell of birth and blood are strong and danger has passed like a shadow over them. Feeling the heaviness in the air that will bring rain at dawn she knows where to head for shelter, sharing the group's knowledge that will bring them there too. Slowly, gently, turning to touch her new baby every few paces, she starts through the night, ears pricked, nostrils wide, drawn towards the safety and comfort of her friends.

Mare and foal touch noses gently, absorbing each other's smell. Mares touch and smell their foals very many times a day. Our ponies do it to us too if they are friendly

Chapter 3

The mustang in your field

For thousands of years this has been the pattern of life for wild horses, whether the earliest ones on the steppes, or the American mustangs and Australian brumbies that bred from escaped tame horses, or the ponies that still keep up the old ways on our British hills and moors. For wild horses, like many other wild animals, life is a balance between escaping danger and injury, keeping fit and well-fed, raising their babies and having time to relax and have a bit of fun too.

But it is not only wild horses that know how to look after themselves. If we people disappeared overnight, taking with us our houses, fences, roads and cars, most of our tame horses would be all right too. For in the back of every horse's mind, be it a tough little Dartmoor bred on the hill or a highly bred and trained dressage horse, there is a store of knowledge that tells it what to eat, where to look for shelter, what to avoid and what to run from. There was a racehorse called Moifaa which in 1904 was shipwrecked off the coast of Ireland while being shipped to Britain from New Zealand. Never having seen sea before, he swam ashore to a barren island and, in totally unfamiliar surroundings, looked after himself perfectly well until he was recaptured by passing fishermen, when he went on to win the Grand National.

In horses that have always lived wild this knowledge is polished and perfected to such a pitch that their lives seem full of idleness and luck: they are almost always at the right place at the right time. Our tame horses usually have little chance to make their own decisions: we don't let them explore or learn the things their minds tell them they should because we are endlessly ordering them about, so they end up rather stupid compared with wild ones. But even in the boring and artificial life we make them lead they go on using this ancient knowledge even when it is completely out of place. They still run from the sound of a rattlesnake even when it is made by the wind rattling the plastic bags their food comes in.

One of the greatest reasons for misunderstandings between us and ponies is that we don't realise how strong this knowledge is. We call them stupid when they spook at things they 'know' are safe. We don't see that the way a horse thinks is not just the way we have taught him to think: it's also the way that horses have had to think for tens of thousands of years, merely to stay alive. That ancient way of thinking is as much a part of being a horse as is the shape of his body. Minds have shapes too, and like bodies the way they work has been tailored for a life that cruelly punishes anything short of perfect. They have to be good at their chosen way of life, or they die.

With an enormous effort of imagination we can put ourselves in the position of wild horses, and see their behaviour coming out in our tame Dobbins. What adds to the difficulty, though, is that our minds have a shape too. It's not as strong as in horses – we depend a lot more on learning – but it is there. If we look at this little story of wild horses, all of which is true enough although it didn't all happen to the same horses on the same day, we can see that we should have behaved quite differently. The store of knowledge in the backs of our minds is suited to a different way of living, though it might be in the same place. Things that are obvious to us are not those that are obvious to them.

Night and day

It seems obvious to us, for instance, to sleep at night and do things in the daytime. We know that owls, foxes, poachers and burglars prowl by night but to most of us that is rather sinister; the backs of our minds say that the decent place to be at night is tucked up safely, asleep for a good long stretch. We strengthen that old knowledge with stories of awful things that happen at midnight: graves open up, ghosts haunt, vampires flit. That's our inheritance.

Horses are different. They eat, doze and move about at any old time of day or night: many's the time I've heard horses playing at three o'clock in the morning. They don't sleep for hours on end: they catnap when they are full and start eating again when they stop feeling full. They do this even when we shut them in stables thinking they'll get a good night's sleep. Instead they get bored and restless at the times they feel they should be moving. If you have ridden horses in the middle of the night you will know they are just as wide awake as in the day. Probably they see better than we do; but they also depend less on their sight. They strain their ears more, sniff the air more, and are more sensitive to the feel of the ground. A horse at night feels like a cat, alert and prowly. Perhaps this is partly because we have to trust his judgement more and he feels that, so he does not ignore his senses and leave the decisions to his rider, which is what we normally ask. He is nearer to being a wild horse and we, for once, must let him be.

At noon on that spring day a group of early people (or, indeed, their modern equivalents) would probably not be asleep in the sun. It wouldn't even be the same kind of group as that of those ponies, although we too do stick together in groups. But you probably wouldn't find one male and several breeding females: it takes a woman a lot more time and effort than a horse to bring up her babies, and usually she has a man all to herself. More likely all the males would have painted themselves and, with a good deal of song and dance and brave talk, gone off hunting together while the women collected roots and leaves. If they noticed the deer, it would not be from the same distance, for our eyes are not as sensitive to movement as horses' eyes are. But the sight of deer wouldn't send them to sleep. Deer are extremely interesting to people: we eat them. We eat horses, too. We are the hunters; they are the hunted.

Hunters and hunted

Vegetarians will object that we can live only on plants, but then some of us live only on animals as do Eskimos and the Masai. We are adaptable. But any biologist will tell you that our teeth, our guts and our eyes instantly show that we are hunters. Sometimes, of course, we get hunted too, but on the whole it is plant-eating animals which get hunted most, for they taste better. But we do know the fear of being hunted. Many people feel it especially in the dark, expecting murderous monsters to spring out from the shadows. For horses, a lot of life is like that. They are terrified of tigers, and they are always on the alert for them.

The fact that there have been no lions or tigers in Britain for a long, long time makes no difference at all, though after a lifetime of not meeting them most old ponies get a bit more sensible about them. The fear is an ancient one, as old as our fear of bears under the bed. I have never met anyone who has found a bear under his bed but there are few people who haven't been afraid of them as children. That ancient fear perhaps arose when we lived in caves and sometimes did come home to a vast shaggy visitor. Like horses, people who didn't have that fear built into the backs of their minds didn't last long.

The family crest of a large house near here bears the motto *Non timeo, sed caveo*: I'm not afraid, but I'm wary. It fits horses perfectly. They are constantly on their guard for signs of tigers, and are suspicious of tigerish noises or places where tigers might hide. Even changing familiar things round may alarm them. Your pony may snort in horror when you restack the wood in the yard, or when he sees a car upside down in the ditch: even when he knows what the things are, he has to make sure they are safe in this curious new arrangement, and that nothing nasty is lurking behind them.

Running away

When we live in a more primitive, natural way, the movements and sounds of other animals interest us more. Out hunting with your spear in hand, you'd whip round at a rustling in the bushes and try to work out what it was. You'd attack a deer or a rabbit, run from a tiger, and ignore a badger. But for a horse there's never any point

The horse's nightmare: a tiger in the bush. When a pony is suddenly startled and makes to run away, it's likely he's seen a tiger or hidden danger that you don't realise

Pete loves to be high on the mountain looking down. He is admiring the view but has flicked one ear back to check on me since I have a strange clicking black box in front of my face

in attacking. He doesn't wait to see what it is: he runs away first, before turning to see whether it's harmless or dangerous. We tend to think that this means ponies are timid, for we would think a person who did the same a hopeless ninny. But it is simply what ponies do. They are wary about any new animal, just in case. Apart from another pony, no animal can be of any help to them.

After that first short, startled sprint, ponies usually turn to work out whether there is any real danger. If there is, they bolt, bunching together for safety. Once they are galloping flat out they seem to stop thinking about anything else except escaping. They get into a running-away frame of mind that feeds on itself: the faster they go the worse they get. What finally stops them is reaching a place they feel safe in, where they can see danger coming.

Resting places

This wariness means that ponies choose their resting places carefully. They like high, open places. Sometimes I turn out Pete and my stallion Max on a huge area of mountain where people think it would take days to find them. But in good weather I can usually see them from five miles away: they're perched on top of a crag, admiring the tigerless wilderness.

When they shelter in bad weather, ponies choose places where their bottoms are protected but they still have a good view. Their natural feeling is always to avoid being shut in, especially in small places where tigers can come leaping in but they can't get out. They don't like going into dark places. We can make stables less awful by putting food in them, but even then the back of a pony's mind tells him that it is no place to be. Many ponies get used to being stabled, especially if they have done it from an early age, but it is still a strain, and if you leave the door open they'll be out again as soon as they have finished eating. Most ponies won't choose to be inside unless there is nowhere else to escape from flies, like a breezy cliff-top. Ponies that have grown up wild, where their natural feelings are strengthened, are often impossible to keep in: they will climb out, smash their way out, or get hysterical. The shape of our minds tells us that caves, dens and stables are lovely safe places to be; but to a horse they are prisons.

Remembering places

It's important for a pony to know which places are safe and which aren't. All ponies, not just wild ones, are brilliant at remembering places where good or bad things have happened. If your pony has had a bad shock you will feel him tense up every time he passes the place it happened. Left to himself he probably wouldn't go anywhere near it. But if he has ever escaped and ended up in some lush garden, or if he has been given an apple outside a house, you will find him trying to turn in there every time you pass.

Pete's memory is extraordinary. We have made many long journeys and once, in a high mountain farm some sixty miles away, we unexpectedly met a girl from our valley who, while we chatted and drank tea, fed Pete bread and carrots. Years later I had a job that involved my riding over the whole of north Wales. Coming out of a Forestry plantation Pete suddenly set off up a steep track in a determined way. Since downhill led to his present field and straight on would eventually lead home, I was intrigued to know what turned him uphill at the end of a long day. Soon we were galloping along narrow tracks, stopping only to let me open gates, until half a mile later we burst out of the trees at the back door of that same farm. He had seen it once, eight years before, approaching from the front. I was astonished, as I'd entirely forgotten the incident and the place. I'm still not sure how he did it, since it was a completely different route from the one we'd first taken, but there was no doubt that he knew exactly what he was doing. He was absolutely triumphant, although he didn't seem to mind that there was no one at home.

Later, on that same job, he turned off a lane and stopped in a puzzled way by a cattle grid that led to a much 'improved' cottage. He seemed annoyed by the grid. Only after five minutes did I realise that we'd stayed there, before the improvements or the grid, many years earlier.

Maps

Pete not only remembers the places he's been: he's got an imaginary map of them in his head, as I have, so that he can get from one to another by ingenious short cuts. I would love to know what his map of Wales looks like, for it's certainly more detailed than mine. All horses can make this kind of map, but most don't get the chance. Pete's maps, though, are much bigger than any normal horse's, for he has travelled far further than even the biggest wild horse range.

The idea of making maps in your head depends on three things: remembering places, remembering paths, and being able to work out directions. Many ponies have found their way home after being moved, often even long distances. Nobody is sure whether they do it by remembering the way or by recognising the landscape. Pete, when he found that farm, may have recognised the mountains and headed for the small hanging valley where the farm lay. People who go hunting often find themselves miles from home, pretty lost, but they know that if they leave it to their horses they'll find the way home. They seem to be able to do it better when the wind's blowing from home, so smell may help.

Once I rode a young mare over the desert in Arizona. We wandered for miles, returning well after dark. We had come over a plain dotted with creosote bushes but without any landmarks. I gave the mare her head. Every now and then she'd drop her head and sniff; then, reassured, she'd jog a bit before stopping to smell again. Sometimes she made a mistake, choosing to go first one way, though uncertainly; then she'd turn back, go to her last checking place and go another way. We arrived home safely and next day I rode the same way again. In the pathless, sandy desert I could clearly see that her homeward hoofprints followed the outward ones, even where we'd wandered around a good bit. She'd tracked herself by smell, following a trail over seven hours old. What impressed me was that she had lived in a pen all her life: I had only just broken her in and it was her first long ride out.

Experiences like these show clearly the strength of a horse's inbuilt knowledge, which is so seldom uncovered in the life we make them lead. Alas, we are usually so bound up in our own ideas about what a horse should or should not do, teaching them to jump or turn in special ways, that we never realise what the horse herself thinks life is about, or where her intelligence might lead.

Paths

Horses get fixed ideas about paths. If you ride over rough ground you find that your pony works out the best way and then keeps to that path for years, only occasionally picking out a variation that improves it. Riding with others, you find that ponies tend to choose to follow each other nose to tail, as would a group of wild horses. Trekking ponies, who do this for years over the same ground, get so set on following the 'right' path that it's nearly impossible to turn them off it, and they hate to leave the string. The same path, preferably following others, feels safe to a pony and you have to make a habit of insisting on variations if you want to stop her getting fixed-minded about it.

Even this has its horse sense. When they run from something startling, ponies raise their heads and tip them back to look at their heels, for that is where threat comes from. But this means they cannot see where they are going, for to see the ground in front of their feet they need to stretch their necks and lower their heads. Watch horses playing at escapes and you will see them with their noses in the air and their eyes rolled back; watch them crossing a ditch and you will see the low head. Knowing every twist and turn in a path so they can gallop it safely in the dark means they can run fast without making mistakes. You probably know that if you put a strange pony into a group who always live in the same field he may cannon into the fence if they bully him, until he has had a chance to learn exactly where it is, for he cannot see it when he is running away from them. Even their love of paths has to do with tigers.

Tigers, snakes and pigs

As well as tigers, horses have an inborn fear of snakes and pigs, though it was not until I rode in country that contained lots of both that I thought about it. A truly wild horse that has never seen a rope before is absolutely terrified of its snakiness, but a tame British horse is also scared by nasty slithery sounds or by the flapping of a bit of plastic on a windy fence. They sound like rattlesnakes, and ring alarm bells in the back of the mind.

Once in Arizona I was given a slightly crazy mare to break in.

She threw herself over backwards if annoyed, which is not what a horsebreaker wants to hear. However, once I had explained things calmly to her she loved being ridden and, rather proud, I set out on her third saddling to show her owner, some five miles away over the mountain. We celebrated Moonie's excellence too long and it was pitch dark by the time we left. Half a mile up the road she stopped dead, all her muscles bunched. She felt like a rumbling volcano. Oh dear, I thought, she wants to go back home and if I don't let her she'll go over backwards. So I waited awhile until she relaxed a little, and pushed again. Back on Vesuvius. But I couldn't give in, so a little while later I tried again. She snorted, and I waited for lift-off; but out of the darkness right in front of her feet a rattlesnake answered. She couldn't have seen it; she hadn't apparently smelt it; she must, I think, have *felt* it was there. But for her wisdom she might be dead and I in a wheelchair. It makes me a lot more sympathetic when horses warn me about plastic bags.

Pigs are also scary, and most tame horses that don't know about pigs are terrified of them. They are also bewildered by donkeys and cows when they haven't seen them before: my donkey once innocently scattered a whole trekking string over the mountain, for they'd taken her to be a pony until she got close enough for her ghastly ears to be obvious. Then they bolted, mostly without their riders. Any large animal might be a threat. Horses that have never seen people before find us particularly horrifying, since we are unlike any other animal and our arms snake out in a sinister fashion, to heaven only knows what length. But the special fear of pigs does have its logic, for apart from their oddness they threaten the feet, and horses cannot bear that.

Feet

Clearly, if your only safety lies in running away you need to be especially careful about your feet, and horses are. It takes a good deal of trust and training before a pony will give you his foot, and even a tame old pony is likely to jump if you grab his foot without warning. Anything that catches the feet, like wire or rope, is likely to panic a horse. Out in the wild a lame horse does not last long, so anything that might possibly endanger the feet is highly suspect. Rivers that might be bottomless or full of alligators, hollow-sounding ramps that might collapse, bogs and marshes that might slow you down, and anything that moves are to be avoided. There is a wonderful scene in the film *Gandhi* where mounted soldiers charge a huge crowd of demonstrators. Gandhi tells the crowd to lie down close together, and the horses refuse to trample over their packed bodies. Horses do sometimes tread on our feet when they can't see them, but if you watch steeplechasing you will often see a whole field of horses gallop straight over a fallen jockey without touching him. It is not kindness, but fear of hurting their feet.

It is this fear about feet that makes ponies unwilling to jump until they learn to trust their riders: what pony would fling himself over a jump he could perfectly well avoid when he cannot even see where his precious feet will land? Jumping is not something that ponies naturally do. Some bold ponies obviously get keyed up about it and seem to enjoy it, but I think they are the sort of characters that would enjoy racing motorbikes, hang-gliding or rock-climbing if they were people: they get a thrill out of getting away with it. Until it gets too serious, it's a game; but it's not a game they invent for themselves.

Games

Like horses, we play games, and like them we play most when we are young or full of energy and well-being. Boys, like colts, are usually rougher than girls (or fillies) and they tend to play with youngsters their own age. Stallions, though, go on playing with all their foals, but as the colts get older and more sure of themselves the games start to get serious. Fathers and sons can get like that, too. But the differences between us start showing up again when we look at the games we play.

I had a rabbit that lived free in my house. He loved to graze the carpet, but he also loved to play. It fascinated me that visitors seldom understood his idea of a game. He would hop and skip bright-eyed in front of them, clearly begging for a romp, but, used to puppies and kittens which are both hunters, most people wiggled their fingers or rolled cottonreels in front of him, expecting him to pounce. He didn't understand that at all. Rabbits don't pounce on things. What he liked was to be chased by roaring monsters, scuttling from one hidey-hole to another so he could show how brilliant he was at escaping. For what young things play at is being grown-up, in a crazy sort of way, and rabbits have to be good at escaping.

We play at dens, at making our own corners snug; we play at using our hands, making and throwing things; and we play at problems, at using our brains, for that is what we are most brilliant at. Horses don't. They play at escapes, like my rabbit. They play at races and twists and turns; they play at bucking off lions that have dropped out of the sky; they conjure up wolves from the breeze in

Colts play-fighting practise the moves they might have to use seriously later if they are to grow up into real wild stallions

their tails and practise running away with one eye on their heels. They never play at dens.

Young horses, like children, also love to explore, to find out where and what things are and how the world works. Sadly, it's a game that many tame horses aren't allowed much chance at. Like us, they like to go out with a gang of friends and in fact for them, like us, all games are best played with friends. One of the most important things about games is not the games themselves but the fact that they are played with friends, for what is being played at is being together, getting on with each other, understanding each other's moods and warnings and learning to live with each other. Apart from running away, it's the most important thing that a horse needs to do. His life depends on being in a group.

Loneliness

Hunter and hunted we may be, but the greatest thing we share with horses is our need of and love for others. For a wild horse it's essential. How could you sleep or eat with those tigers in the bushes? Ponies hate to be alone. Many of them have to learn to live alone, but you may have noticed that your pony is more pleased to see you when he's alone than when he's kept with other ponies. He needs your company. This is rather flattering, but it means there is a lot of the day when he's lonely, and you probably know what that feels like.

Some ponies cannot get used to being alone. Mangas Colorado, a great-hearted, spirited piebald pony, could never be left by himself, even when he was over forty. He would jump fences, smash gates, uproot posts and break ropes in his desperation. If he was shut in a stable you would find him dripping with sweat, eyes rolling, unable to eat or sleep, and he'd run straight over you when you opened the door. He was an extreme case, and most ponies get depressed rather than hysterical by loneliness, but all ponies eat better, sleep better and are generally far happier when they are kept with a friend.

Sam, a five-year-old mustang stallion, had never seen people until he was rounded up. At first he was terrified even of the smell of my clothes hanging on the side of his pen, but after a week he'd accepted me enough to be released into the field where I was camping. A few hours later he wandered up to me, yawned, and lay down. Remembering the tame horses that had come to me when they felt ill, I thought he was colicky; but when I looked down he was already fast asleep. Being a truly wild horse, he'd never slept alone, and he needed someone to watch over him while he did. The poor fellow was exhausted after a week without a decent lie-down sleep.

Like us, horses feel safer when there are others around. They like to be members of a group, and they have strong ideas of who is in their group and who isn't. It takes time for a newcomer to get accepted as a member of a group, just as a playground gang at school will not easily accept a new child. She has to hang around the outside, getting driven away again and again, until they finally realise she is here to stay. After that, they get worried when she does not turn up, and start looking for her.

Exploring a difficult track up Snowdon while on a long journey with Pete and
Dolly. Pete was watching where he was going but Dolly, who had never been
up a mountain before, was so frightened that she followed him too closely, and
kept stumbling. Finally I tied her up and went on with Pete, but when we
returned she'd been so frightened of being abandoned in this terrible place
that she was sweating and shaking. Travelling with your pony brings you much
closer together (Photo: Jane Turner)

Friends

In our need for company, our ties with our family and our liking
for our friends, we are very like horses. They too have special
friends whom they like to be with all the time. People are sometimes
annoyed by the way a pony gets upset when his friend is taken
away, but we do the same thing when we are separated from people
we love. Since ponies live with their friends all the time, one of the
ways we can get really close to them is by living with them. When
you travel a long distance with a horse, living, eating and sleeping
with him for weeks on end, you fit into his idea of what a friend
is. Tschiffely, on his great ride through the Americas, found that
he did not need to tether his horses at night: they would not leave
him. Like Sam, they needed him to protect them.

But it is especially when you travel with a horse in country new
to both of you that you start realising more differences between us.
Even when you begin to think like a pony, seeing the lurking tigers
and the dangers to the precious feet, you still miss out sometimes.
For their eyes are not ours; their ears hear things we don't; they
have whiskers, and a sense of smell far beyond ours. Their senses
are different.

Chapter 4

Senses

'There are more things in heaven and earth, Horatio, than are dreamt of in your philosophy,' says Hamlet. He might have added that there are more things to sense than we people dream of, too. Many animals can see, feel, hear or sense things that we can't. Our sense organs – eyes, ears, noses, skin – are like little peepholes on the world: they see only a bit of it. Bees can see ultraviolet light: whites that all look white to us look like twenty different colours to them. Electric eels can sense other animals moving in the electric fields they throw around themselves; pigeons can sense the earth's magnetism, which they use in homing; pit vipers hunt by 'seeing' heat from mice in the dark; salmon can smell their own rivers. And horses have senses that are sometimes better than ours, sometimes worse, and sometimes just different.

Eyes

Horses' eyes are very different from ours. For a start they are set on the sides of their heads, not on the front. If you want to judge distances very exactly, which is what a hunter needs to do if he is to pounce on another animal, you need both eyes pointing in the same direction. Tigers, owls, dogs and cats all have eyes that point forwards. This, of course, means that they can't see behind themselves, but it doesn't worry them much since they are not afraid of being attacked from behind.

For animals that are hunted, though, attack from behind is exactly what they are worried about. In fact, it worries them more than being able to judge distances. Most animals that are hunted, like horses, have eyes on the sides of their heads so that they can

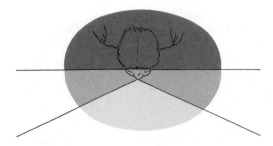

a) How much you can see. Without rolling your eyes, you can see to the side with each eye. You can see a large area in front with both eyes, so you can judge distances. You can't see behind yourself without turning your head

b) How much your pony can see. Without turning his head, he can see almost all round himself. Right in front of his nose he is blind, but further in front he can see with both eyes. He can't see behind himself, or his sides, without turning his head. If he is tied up, he may be nervous of you doing things where he can't see you unless you stay close to him so that he can feel you, and talk to him so he is comforted

see almost all round themselves. If a horse tips his head up and to one side he can see the backs of his heels too, but he can't see so well in front then.

Field of vision. Try working out how much you can see. Close your left eye, look straight ahead with your right eye, hold up one finger and move it slowly round your head. You'll want to roll your eye to follow your finger, but try to look straight ahead. Your finger disappears when it's about level with your right ear; on the other side it disappears when it's about a foot in front of your left

c) How much a cat can see. Like you, a cat can see a large area in front with both eyes, so he can judge where to pounce accurately when he is hunting. His eyes bulge out more than yours, so he can see further behind with each eye. Both you and a cat have typical hunter's eyes

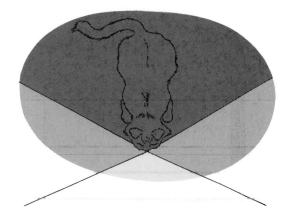

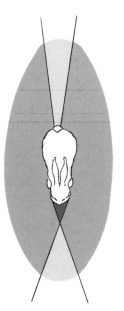

d) How much a rabbit can see. Like a horse, a rabbit can see only a small area in front with both eyes. But because his eyes bulge more than a horse's he can also see behind his tail with both eyes. This means he can judge exactly how near a hunter is to his tail, and can dash to one side just as he's about to be caught. A horse's eyes work like a rabbit's, not like yours. He is not a hunter, but is always on the look-out in case he is being hunted

▢	– can be seen with both eyes
▨	– can be seen with one eye
▦	– can't be seen at all

shoulder, or ten o'clock from your nose. The part you can see is called the field of vision. You can also see from about level with your forehead to level with your chest. If you roll your eye sideways, or up, you can see further in that direction but not so far in the other.

You will also notice that you can see your finger clearly only when it's in front of you, in the middle of the field of vision. Elsewhere it's fuzzy, but when you see something fuzzy out of the corner of your eye you immediately want to roll your eye to see it clearly.

When you open your left eye as well you can now see further to the left, though only fuzzily; but something else happens, too. Straight ahead, things don't necessarily look sharper but they look deeper. They take on shape, not looking so flat. This is because you can see things in depth only when you look at them from two angles at once, that is, with both eyes at once.

No matter how much you roll your eyes you cannot see any of your face except the end of your nose; nor can you see your chin, your neck or your head. To see behind you, you have to turn your head; but you can't turn it right round as an owl can.

Horses have a much bigger field of vision than we do. Of course, their necks are so long and bendy that they can move their heads more than we can, but even when they face straight forwards they can see almost all round themselves. The only bit they can see with two eyes is straight ahead. Like us, they turn their heads or roll their eyes to try to look straight at something they've seen in the fuzzy bit of their field of vision.

Ponies can't see behind themselves unless they turn their heads. Unlike us, they can't see anything right in front of their noses either, for about a metre or so; exactly how far depends on whether their eyes are more on the sides of their heads or are more forward-looking. Most ponies don't like it if you walk straight towards them from in front, because you disappear when you get close: they back away, or turn their heads to one side. If you're trying to catch them it looks as if they're trying to escape, but they're only trying to see you properly. If you stand still right in front of a pony's nose and stroke his face he will often get a shock, because he can't see your hand. That is why you are taught to go up to a pony from the side, and to put your hand on his neck where he can see it coming.

Ponies can't see their noses. Sometimes when you offer a titbit when a pony is tied up he will ignore it because he hasn't seen it: often he will cock his head sideways to squint down with one eye, but sometimes he will pull back so that he can see your hand with both eyes. If you keep moving your hand when you are trying to hand-feed a horse he may get quite annoyed because he keeps aiming at the place he last saw it.

It may seem surprising that a horse can't see what he is eating, but you can't see your mouth either. Watch a baby trying to feed himself and you will realise that you had to learn where your mouth is; if you watch a young foal you will see he's not quite sure where his nose ends.

When a pony is walking with her head in a normal position, nose level with her chest, she can see the ground about 4 metres ahead

The Steed, who had been nuzzling Rick a moment before, has just smelt his apple and turned her head away so that she can see it. You can see that both her eye and ear are intent on it, and her nostrils are flared

of her clearly and in depth. But she cannot see the ground as she steps on it at all. She can see the sides of the track she is walking on, but only fuzzily. So if she is worried by things on the path, or beside it, she will want to move her head so she can see them clearly. If she wants to see exactly where to put her feet, as on a stony or boggy bit, she needs to drop her head low. If she wants to see something in the hedge she needs to cock her head sideways, or turn her head, or even to jump on one side while she is turning her head. We call this shying.

Now, if you are the sort of person who rides along with a head full of dreams and your hands stiff, not paying much thought to what bothers your pony, you will probably be annoyed if she suddenly tries to pull the reins out of your hands, or leaps sideways. The pony, though, is only trying to see properly, and if she is a nervous sort of pony she will feel even more nervous if every time she tries to look at things she gets first of all a jab in the mouth and then a telling off. You do not need to ride with a completely loose rein, but you do need to hold the rein lightly, letting it run through your fingers if the pony asks to be able to see properly. Most ponies, for instance, will not cross a stream without having a good peer at it first, to make sure of the footing and check there are no alligators, and for this they need to put their heads low. What you have to be good at is being quick to gather up the reins again as the pony's head comes up, so that you still have control if she decides to turn away.

Focusing.   The second great difference between our eyes and a pony's is the way they focus. Hold up your finger about 10 inches in front of you. You can see it clearly, wrinkles, dirt under the nail and all. But without moving your head or eyes you can now focus on the top of a hillside miles away. When you do this your finger becomes just a pinkish blob. When you look at it again the horizon goes fuzzy. You cannot keep far things and near things in focus at the same time. Also, you can focus only on what is straight in front of your eye. This is not to do with depth: you can read with one eye, but the writing needs to be lined up with the middle of it. This is because the most sensitive part of the eye in daylight is a spot right in the middle (at night it isn't: you may have noticed that you can see stars more clearly when you look to one side of them).

A horse does not focus like we do. In fact, although this is difficult to test, it seems that ponies really do not focus as sharply as we do anyway; they could not read even if they were clever enough because they do not see the detail. But when a horse sees something far in the distance he uses a different part of the eye to the bit he uses when something is close. Roughly, when his head is high, distant things are sharpest, when it is middling then middling things are sharpest, and when it is low the ground in front of him is sharpest. But of course he can tilt his eyes by moving his nose in or out: if he sticks his nose out while his head is low then he is looking at middle-distant things. If he sticks his nose out when his head is high, so that his head is almost flat, he can see his back and his heels.

All this is far more difficult to understand when it's written down than it is when you learn by watching a pony. It's also made even more complicated by the fact that ponies can roll their eyes. But if you pay attention whenever a pony is interested in something, and watch his head position, you will gradually begin to be able to tell immediately what he is looking at.

It is important for you to know what your pony is looking at because many of the difficulties and misunderstandings that people have with horses come from the differences in our eyes. Literally

This pony in a trekking yard is looking at the photographer with one eye but down at his empty feed box with the other. The pony on the right would be able to see us if he rolled his eye back, but he is looking at the other ponies instead.

The hay nets have been tied very low down; if the ponies pawed they would get their feet caught

hundreds of times I have seen ponies fighting desperately to be allowed to get a good look at something that frightened them, while the person holding or riding them was fighting equally desperately, thinking they were trying to escape. Often a pony is not frightened by what we think, but something completely different: he may refuse to go into a stable because of the wheelbarrow outside, or into a trailer because of the plastic sack beside it. If you cannot tell what it is he is looking at, or do not give him the freedom to see, he is quite right not to trust you, for you may be leading him blindly into far worse dangers.

Movement. The third great difference between horses' eyes and ours is that they see movement far better than ours do, and detail not so well. Once, out with Pete in the autumn, I walked and let him wander ahead up a rocky path. Suddenly he stopped, staring intently at a pile of dead leaves about five metres ahead of him. After we'd waited for what seemed like hours the top leaf moved and a minute worm crawled out from underneath. I suppose he'd seen it move before, in a way that he knew wasn't the breeze. There is no way I should have noticed it. I can live without worms being pointed out to me, but he has shown me hundreds of other things that I never should have seen: boring ones like tiny tractors crawling over distant horizons, or sheep moving on a mountain five miles away, but also wonderful ones like foxes crouching in the bracken, deer camouflaged under dark trees, wild goats perched on high crags, snakey-headed badgers on our evening prowls, and once a pair of mating moles. Many wild animals freeze the moment they see you, trusting that their cleverly coloured coats will hide them; but Pete's eyes are so quick that he sees even that moment of freezing. He stops and stares, but often, I think, the camouflage does fool him and his eyes are not sharp enough to see the shape of the animal. It takes my eyes, which would not see there was something there unless he pointed it out to me, to be able to tease out the outline of the animal. If it were not for him I should not have seen half the wildlife that I have.

One reason that I do see those hedgehogs, stoats, foxes and deer is that I allow Pete to stop and stare. (Also, of course, they're not as afraid as if I were on foot, for what they see and hear is a horse, not a human.) Many people think their ponies are being naughty or silly when they stop, and kick them on angrily. They ask their ponies to be machines that notice nothing. Pete is very funny when other people ride him: if he points out something and they ignore him he turns round and nudges their feet. Of course they don't understand that either, which annoys him. I don't think it is 'bad discipline' to let him look at things that interest him, and he has realised that tractors don't interest me although foxes do. He is also sensitive and intelligent enough to know when I don't want him to stop, in a show or competition for instance. In just such a way does a foal learn from his mother what is genuinely interesting: when he races back to her after being startled by a butterfly she ignores him, but when he sees a wolf she's quick to call him to her and gallop off. He learns, too, to stick beside her and behave himself on the march. Ponies are not stupid, and it must be awful to be treated as stupid by people who are half-blind and narrow-minded.

Night sight.   Ponies can see well in the dark, as you might expect of animals that spend half the night wandering about, though like us they take time to adjust to darkness. Coming from a brightly lit stable at night they are as blind as we are for a few minutes, and they hate to have a torch shone straight at their heads because it dazzles them. If you have to work round a horse at night with a torch, don't shine it in his eyes; hang it up. In daytime, try to light a dark place before asking a pony to go in; for instance, open the jockey door of a trailer before trying to lead a pony.

I can see extremely well in the dark (for a person) but ponies seem to see far better than I can, although they too get confused in bright moonlight sometimes. On very dark nights, or under trees where I can see almost nothing, they are still quite confident, but they may be using other senses or their brilliant memories to help them.

Colours.   Scientists have proved that ponies definitely do see colours. All the colours we see are in a rainbow: red, orange, yellow, green, blue, indigo, violet. Other animals, mostly insects, see bands of colour beyond the violet, where we see only blank; but they see blank where we see red. Horses, it seems, don't see red either, and probably not violet, but they do see all the colours in the middle. At night they can't see colours any more than we can.

One thing that puzzles me about horses' eyesight concerns sinister rocks. In these craggy mountains there are certain rocks that make almost all horses snort and shy. Most of them are about the size of a pig and of pale stone, though not white quartz. I have known horses to be so frightened as to run away from them in panic. It must have something to do with the light, since they're not always terrifying. It may be that they are animal-sized but not moving, for sometimes a big log, a scoop of mud left by the ditching machine, or a hump of silage will surprise them too.

Hearing

If you've arranged to meet a friend with your ponies you'll know that your pony can hear much better than you. He starts to neigh and jump up and down long before you can hear the clatter of hoofs. As well as hearing fainter noises than you can, he can also hear sounds too high or low for your ears.

Since ponies can move their ears in most directions they can tell exactly where a sound is coming from, and by turning to point both ears at it they can concentrate on it and cut out other noises in the background. This is particularly useful for listening to faint sounds that might mean danger: rustlings and slitherings in bushes, for instance. Rattles alarm horses, but they quickly get sharp at telling the difference between rattles made by buckets and other, more sinister, kinds of rattles.

It is easy to train a horse to word commands, as long as you remember to say them in the same tone of voice, and ponies have no difficulty in recognising different voices, whether human or horse.

One reason for horses being alarmed when we can see nothing wrong may be that they are hearing noises we aren't. A young stallion I rode in Portugal, on his first ride off the farm, would suddenly stop, neigh, and go prancing forward for no apparent reason. In Portugal many animals wear bells, which he could hear several hundred yards further away than I could. Since he came from a horse farm he naturally thought that bells always meant mares. After a couple of hours and many disappointments he realised that sheep and goats wear smaller, tinklier bells than cows and horses, while I learned that every time he got mysteriously excited I would hear bells a minute later.

Smells

Many animals 'talk' to each other with smells. If you watch an ant-heap you will see the ants touching each other all the time with their feelers, which is where they keep their noses. By the smell of another ant they know where it comes from, what it has been doing, and what they need to do next. Smells are their language.

Ponies use smell-language too, though not as much as ants. They are far more sensitive to smell than we are. Their noses are huge, with big nerves running from them. But as well as their ordinary noses they have another way of smelling, which they use only sometimes. This is called the Jacobson's organ, and it is a little hollow deep inside the nose. Smells can't usually get into it, but if the pony takes a deep breath, rolls his top lip back over his nostrils to stop the air escaping and then pushes the air backwards, it is forced into the hollow. You will see ponies do this when they taste something new; people say the pony is laughing, or call it the 'stallion smile' because stallions do it when they smell a mare, but he is actually tring to work out what the smell is. It is called *Flehmen* in German; oddly, there's no word for it in English.

Smells tell ponies a lot about each other: they always smell each other's noses when they first meet. What they learn, though, we don't know. They can certainly tell from one whiff whether they are meeting a mare, a gelding or a stallion, and whether or not a mare is in season; but if you watch them you will see that they go on sniffing carefully for some time and can apparently decide whether they will be friends, enemies, or just ignore each other.

Some people say that you, too, should smell the nose of a pony if you want to be friends with him, but that is not as sensible as it sounds. Young or wild ponies do want to smell your face, and it is safe to let them (but beware that they usually move on to trying to eat your hair). But shoving your face into the nose of an old tame pony who knows that people don't usually behave like that is asking to have your face bitten, especially if he is a grumpy riding-school pony. I have been particularly asked to say this by a number of doctors who have seen children with terrible injuries. As a rule, then, don't offer to smell a pony's nose, but if he wants to smell yours you may let him. If you want to make friends with a new pony, he will be most interested if you wear clothes that already smell of pony. Stand quietly beside him for a few moments, then stroke his neck and scratch the bottom of his mane and his withers, quite hard. Ponies do this only to their friends, and he will know you are trying to be friendly.

Ponies recognise each other's smell, and it is the way that mares recognise their foals. Smell also seems to be one of the things that keeps a group together. All the ponies in one group roll in the same spot, so that they all get the same smell. A new pony is not accepted as a member of the group until he has rolled there often enough to smell right.

Since smell is so important in recognising each other, ponies are extremely interested when they come across pony-smells. Dung is especially fascinating to them: they can tell whether it comes from a mare, gelding or stallion, how long ago, whether the pony was

This stallion, smelling a mare, rolls his top lip back over his nostrils to stop the air escaping as he forces it down into the back of his nose

This friendly colt wants to touch Elli gently and smell her breath. This is fine if the horse asks to do it; but don't offer to smell a horse's nose first in case he is bad-tempered. Ruca, the colt's mother, loves to stand close to Elli like a real friend. A Lusitano mare from Portugal, she had been harshly treated and was nervous of people; but when she realized that Elli was kind and gentle she followed her around like a dog and would try to stop her from leaving the field. Elli made a long journey with Ruca in Portugal and brought her back to Britain on a ship across the Bay of Biscay in a storm, so she and Ruca are very close

frightened or in season, what she had been eating and maybe a lot more too. You will often find your pony smelling the top of a gate which has been used by other riders, and many ponies will insist on smelling another pony's tack before they let you put it on them. They will go into a dirty trailer more easily than a clean one, since they can smell that ponies have been there before; and some ponies insist on peeing on a clean bed. It makes it smell like home.

Ponies can track each other or themselves by smell, and they can track other animals too. The first time Pete and I went into a certain huge forest he seemed very puzzled by smells on the ground, and kept peering into the trees after sniffing them. I didn't know he was smelling deer, and he didn't know such animals existed, but

Pete smells his ways over mountain bogs

after he'd seen them a couple of times he would, on finding the smell again, set off in a determined way, sniffing carefully, until he tracked them down. For some reason he seemed as delighted by deer as I was, and although they were quite wild, being hunted, he managed to find some two or three times every day. He also smells out the paths that sheep use to cross large bits of mountain bog.

Taste

We don't know a lot about a pony's sense of taste, but ponies are certainly extremely suspicious about new foods. Since they can't be sick this is quite sensible, though it does not look sensible when you see half-starved wild ponies refusing to eat any of the foods that we know they will like: oats, barley, maize, nuts, apples, carrots, bread and even hay. Most ponies like sweet things, like fruit (Max adores grapes, sucking them like gobstoppers with a dreamy look in his eye), treacle and mints. They don't like bitter tastes, and are highly sensitive to them. Most plant poisons are bitter, especially when fresh, so this may be why. Ponies rarely eat fresh poisonous plants unless they are desperately hungry, but they do sometimes eat dried poisonous plants.

What is surprising is the way that ponies can work out which is the bad-tasting bit in a mixed mouthful of food. Watch your pony grazing a mixed hedgerow and you may see him spit out part of a mouthful and go on munching the rest. Before there were paste wormers, we used to give ponies special wormer nuts, mixing them into a feed of normal nuts, and clever or fussy ponies would always pick them out. We once tested this, counting 35 wormer nuts into thousands of good nuts. Twenty minutes later we had 34 wormer nuts and a smug-looking pony: maddening, but brilliant.

It is a good idea to get your pony keen on treacle, for the taste is so strong that it disguises other tastes, for instance medicines. Thick treacle sandwiches are a great way to give medicine powders.

Whiskers

Again we don't know much about what a pony's whiskers tell her, though we do know that the nerves from the whiskers are big and seem important. A bearded friend of mine tells me that his moustache is sensitive even to the slightest touch, but he wasn't good at telling what he was touched by. Ponies, to judge from their nerves, are much more sensitive than he. Go back to watching your pony on mixed grazing and you will see that although he does sometimes eat a nasty-tasting plant, more often he will push it aside with his nose so he never takes it in his mouth at all. Possibly his whiskers tell him the shape and softness of the plant before he bites it. Once I was watching Welsh mountain ponies, which are canny and clever, grazing on a slope solidly covered in bluebells. They flipped the bluebell leaves up with their noses and snatched the tiny blades of grass underneath, and though I can't be sure I thought that it was their whiskers that helped them do that.

Certainly a horse's whiskers tell him where the end of his nose is. They are also sensitive to wind and puffs of air, so that when two ponies meet and blow into each other's noses their whiskers tell them exactly what is going on.

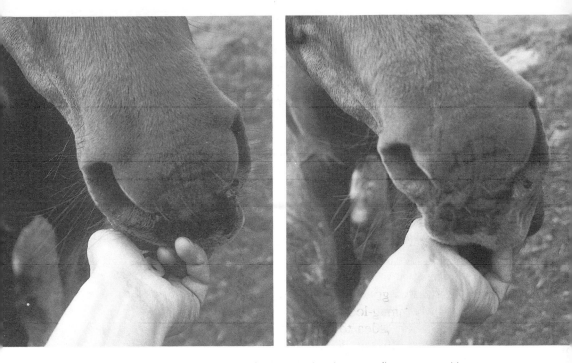

Pete smells the mint in my hand and feels exactly where my fingers are with his whiskers and nose . . .

. . . then he wiggles his nose to open my fingers one by one. This is not a sensible way to feed a pony unless you know he is gentle and not greedy: offer him food on the flat of your hand instead

Don't shave off your pony's whiskers, even for a show, no matter what you are told. To him it is like your putting his eyes out: cruel and in a way blinding. If we all stop doing it then judges will have to get used to it.

Touch

The sense of touch doesn't work quite the same as other senses. As long as there is a noise, you go on hearing it; as long as there is light, you go on seeing. But if you touch something, you stop feeling it unless you keep moving your finger over it. If this weren't so you'd be constantly irritated by your clothes.

Remember this especially when you are riding, for it means that if you keep a dead hand on the rein, or your legs are always against the pony's sides, he soon stops feeling it and becomes dead himself. Always ride lightly, for then your pony can feel the tiniest change in what you are doing.

Some parts of the body are much more sensitive to touch than others. Your fingers, lips and the soles of your feet are far more sensitive than your knees or elbows. Ponies' noses and lips are their most sensitive parts. Pete can open my fingers one by one with his nose, and many clever ponies can undo bolts, latches and even complicated knots by feel. You will notice when you are brushing your pony that she is more ticklish under her belly than on her back, and that there are some bits, like the withers and rump, which she enjoys having scratched. You will also notice that some ponies are altogether more sensitive than others: thin-skinned horses like Thoroughbreds and Arabs must be handled more carefully than solid cobs. Almost all ponies prefer to be handled softly, though I have known a few that were terribly ticklish and could not bear to be touched lightly. Pete hates his flanks to be stroked gently, which is unfortunate since many tiny children seem to want to do exactly that.

When your touch irritates a pony he behaves as if you were a fly: he whisks his tail at you, or wriggles his skin under your hand. He probably will pull a face, too, wrinkling up his nose and looking disgusted. If the saddle is rubbing, for instance, you will find he has a sensitive spot on his back long before it can be seen.

But all ponies like to be touched in the right way, and they touch their friends a good deal. Work out exactly what pleases your pony most. It varies with different ponies. If your pony doesn't love being groomed you are probably using the wrong brush or touch for her. Max likes having his bottom scratched, and he terrorises strangers by galloping up to them and whipping round to offer them his back end. Naturally, they think he's about to kick, which never enters his head. He likes having his withers and neck scratched hard and his face rubbed. Pete likes to have his face fondled much more softly. Try standing right in front of your pony and rubbing his cheeks gently. Many ponies get quite dreamy, perhaps because they are trusting you so much in letting you stand in their blank space. Some ponies like to be rubbed on the forehead between the eyes, and if they push their foreheads into your hand you can be sure they trust you. Once I rode a great distance on Pete with a young mare, Dolly, as a packpony. Twenty times a day she would trot up beside me and press her forehead into my outstretched hand, like a small child running up to take my hand for a moment.

Massage relaxes ponies; if you have ever had a massage you will know it makes you feel quite jellylike. Massage your pony especially along her neck and back, rather as if you were kneading bread or plasticine. The best movement is rubbing your flat hand in circles,

Seren was badly beaten while being 'broken in' and when I first had her she was so frightened that she was stiff all over. I had to massage her daily for ten days before she relaxed enough to be ridden. Here Jane, her present owner, massages her neck to loosen it. Seren's saggy mouth, soft eye and relaxed neck show that she is in a dreamy, gentle state

using your fingers to push the flesh towards the palm of your hand. Your movements should be smooth and rhythmic; it helps if you sing a song to work to. It is difficult to describe in words, especially briefly, but you will learn by experimenting with your pony what makes her relax. Start at the withers, work up her neck, down her back, and watch her body droop as she becomes almost hypnotised. The great value of this is that you can then use massage to relax and soothe a pony when she is, say, in a new place, or nervous, miserable or sick, or just to make her feel contented and loved.

Shaking

Ponies are more sensitive than we are to feelings they get through their feet. They can feel a train coming long before we can and, as Black Beauty pointed out, the shaking terrifies them until they have got used to it. I have never seen ponies in an earthquake, but it's said they feel it coming and try to run away. Other feelings of the ground trembling come when a pony puts his feet on something hollow, like a ramp or bridge, or on a quaking bog. But they may be able to sense more than that, too. Moonie, when she sensed that rattlesnake in the dark, may have felt through her feet that the ground ahead was different. A blind man once told me that he could use the feelings he got through his feet in this way. He'd been born blind, and he said that made his other senses sharper than those of a sighted person.

Size

Ponies know exactly how tall and wide they are, although they can't see their backs or sides without turning their heads. When we're riding them they can't see us, and they don't always realise that bits of us, like our heads or knees, stick out so much. Young ponies, in particular, sometimes get a shock if you ride under a tree and let its leaves hit your head: they don't realise what has happened and the noise sounds like something horrible dropping from the tree on to their backs. They are also likely to squash your knees on gateposts.

Ponies often get accused of bashing their riders into trees or walls in order to get rid of them. Most of them, I'm sure, do this thoughtlessly, not deliberately. You can't expect a pony to look out for you when he can't see you: you must look out for yourself. Anyway, you can bend low enough to get under any branch that most ponies would go under. But I must admit that there are a few clever, nasty-tempered ponies that do hope to leave you hanging in the branches.

Many of the things ponies sense, then, are unknown to us. Yet if we watch our ponies carefully we can see that they have sensed something and whether it pleases or scares them. This is part of the art of learning horse language.

Chapter 5

Language

Do ponies really have a language? They certainly don't have one like ours, but like all animals that live in groups they are clever at understanding one another. They are clever at understanding us too, or we shouldn't be able to do so much with them.

What do we mean by language? The words on this paper are language to you and me, and we understand what they mean. To a Russian they are a language he can't understand. But to an Amazonian Indian they are just squiggles. He would have no idea that they have anything to do with talking, although he can 'read' the forest where he lives in a way that you haven't dreamed of.

Language is the way we understand each other's meaning. There are different sorts of language. There are the words you say, which of course sound quite different depending on what part of the world you live in. There are the squiggles you write, which again are different depending on where you are. There are sign languages, like those that deaf and dumb people, bookies and American Indians use. These depend on the group you belong to, too.

In these types of languages, sounds and signs mean exact things like *apple* or *walking* or *afterwards*. As far as we know, people are the only animals that use thousands of words. Chimpanzees can learn simple sign language, and other animals including ponies learn to understand a couple of dozen words or signs, but they don't remember more than that.

Body language

Another kind of language is body language. This is what you are using when you see your mother coming down the street and know what kind of a mood she is in long before she speaks to you. You can tell by the way she moves. You may not know why she is in that mood, and she may not realise what she is saying. She may even try to hide it, if for instance she's just had a row with your father and doesn't want you to know; but you can tell anyway. It's easy to lie when you speak, write or sign, but it's terribly difficult for most people to lie in body language. Actors, who seem to be able to fake it, say they can't: they have to feel the feelings of the person they're acting, and the right body language then comes out.

Body language is about moods and feelings. You can't say *apple* or *afterwards* but you can in one 'word' say things that sound complicated in other kinds of language, like; 'I'd be happy to go that way but I don't like the mood you're in,' or 'You come one step further and I'll whack you,' or 'I'm exhausted and I'd like to lie down but this place makes me nervous.' Most of these messages look much the same the world over: a nervous Chinese man does the same sorts of things as a nervous Italian, but they may use different sign language to back up their body language.

Ponies are brilliant at body language, better than we are: we're often so busy listening to words that we don't notice what bodies say. As you can see, most of my body language is about the way I feel. I may say I'm happy, sad or lonely, or I may show how I feel about you or anything else. These are the things that ponies in a group need to know if they are to get on together. They do not need to know who is on the television tonight, when the next bus goes, or the words of the latest pop song. Their language serves better than ours, perhaps, for they do not have wars, murders, or even most of the smaller misunderstandings that we do.

If you are to understand your pony you will have to learn his language. Sometimes you will be reading messages sent from one pony to another, like a spy tapping a telephone. Sometimes your pony will deliberately give you messages as if you were another pony, for instance by nickering to you, or warning that he doesn't like what you are doing. Sometimes his body will show how he is feeling without him deliberately giving you that message: a sick pony looks the same whether you are there or not. But the more you can understand of his signs and body language the better you will understand him, and the happier he will feel.

Pony-talk

Ponies 'talk' in several ways: with the shape of the whole body; with their ears, tails and the expressions on their faces; with movements of their skin, tails or feet; by moving their whole bodies; with their voices; with smells. They speak the same language to us as they do to other ponies, and it's the same the world over. But some ponies also develop special signs that they use to their owners, just as friends sometimes use a word, or make up one, to have a special meaning that only they understand.

Shape of the body

Roughly, the more exciting his body looks, the more excited a pony is. When a stallion comes into a show-ring prancing and dancing so he catches your eye, it's because he's excited. When a pony's half-asleep he looks bored, boring and dull. This is not just chance. It is also a signal to other ponies in the group. That show stallion *wants* to be noticed: he wants to warn off other stallions and catch the mares' eyes. The sleepy pony doesn't: he'd prefer to stay asleep, and his outline tells others that it's safe for them to sleep, too.

Excitement. When a pony is excited, his head and tail go up, and when he moves he lifts his feet higher than usual. But there are many different reasons for his excitement: because it's a glorious

This stallion has just spotted a mare in the distance, and his whole body says 'Look at ME!' His high head, high tail and high steps make him an exciting horse to see. Every muscle in tense, but he is in control of himself. He will bounce forward slowly, then stop for a better look before bounding on again. As well as staring, he flares his nostrils and pricks his ears at the mare. Nothing else matters to him. His tense neck and tight mouth mean that if you were riding him he wouldn't feel the bit day and he feels full of fun and energy; because he's seen another pony and wants to meet it; because he's seen a tiger, or thinks he has; because he's puzzled and interested by what's in front of him. To decide which is the right reason you have to look more closely at the other signals he's giving and how he's moving.

Fear. A pony that's frightened is tense as well as high. His muscles tighten up just as yours do, ready to explode into action. With practice you can see this stiffness anywhere in his body, but the first places to look are in his mouth and neck. His mouth goes so tight that, like the stallion in the story, he cannot go on eating the

This pretty Welsh pony at a sale is terrified. He stands perfectly still, frozen, with his neck so tense that the muscles stand out and his nose pokes out. His eye is wide, trying to take in everything, and his turned-back ears show that he fears attack from behind. He feels himself surrounded by danger but isn't sure where it's going to come from.

If you were riding this pony you'd find that he would stand stock-still and stiff, and when you urged him on he'd suddenly leap forward in panic. His mouth and neck are so stiff you wouldn't be able to control him. When a pony is as frightened as this you need to calm and relax him before asking him to do anything.

The pony behind is showing exactly the same signs

grass in it. Often you see people trying to offer food to a frightened pony whose mouth is far too tight to be able to take it, for instance when trying to bribe him into a trailer. When you are riding you can feel a frightened pony's mouth tighten up on the bit so he no longer feels it.

When a pony's neck goes stiff he cannot swing his head round. Instead he has to roll his eyes, or jump about, if he wants to look anywhere but straight ahead of himself. When you pull on the rope or rein he does not give to it, but stiffens up even more, and the more you pull the more he pulls back. The next time this happens, try getting rid of the stiffness instead of fighting it: put your hand on his neck and rub him. At first he will feel as hard as a board, but all of a sudden he will relax, rub back against you, and be able to move his head and neck freely. As soon as he has relaxed he is much more likely to behave sensibly, look at things properly, and be ready to listen to you when you ask him gently.

Sometimes this stiffness in the neck stops a pony going forward, for she cannot see where her feet are going. This frightens her more and she gets even more stiff-necked, high-headed and 'obstinate'. This can be particularly difficult when you want to go down a bank or into a river and the pony has got tense about it. Kicking and

A frightened pony stiffens his neck and back, often watching his heels. He tightens his mouth, lays his ears back, and flares his nostrils to smell danger. He is ready to spring forward although he can't really see where he is going.

When you are riding a frightened pony you have little control with the reins, for his neck and mouth are so stiff that he cannot feel the bit until you pull so hard that you hurt him. This of course frightens him more. Sit well down in the saddle with your legs relaxed: if you tense up and lean forward he will run away. Relax your hand and rub his neck until you feel him start to loosen up. It is often rough handling of the reins that frightens ponies in the first place

shouting will only make her more tense and less able to see; what you need to do is to get her to relax her neck and drop her head, then she will be able to work out her footing.

A frightened pony moves in a stiff, jerky way. You see this best when a pony is startled. Instantly she snaps into a high-headed, high-tailed shape that calls other ponies' attention to her. If they do not take any notice, she will take a few high, jerky steps forward and stop again. These queer movements quickly catch the eye, and other ponies turn to look at the danger. If they decide it's not a threat, their relaxed bodies show the frightened pony that there is nothing to fear; but if they, too, think there is a tiger they will tense up, whirl round, and all will gallop off together.

Because they are always on the look-out for danger, ponies are very sensitive to signs of tension, both in other ponies and in us. When you want to do something with your pony that you think may frighten her, it is a good idea to bring along an older, unworried

When fear erupts into panic a horse simply fights until he escapes or falls over. He does not seem to see, hear or feel, and may do himself terrible damage by crashing into anything around, including you. If he falls over, sit on his head or neck as quickly as possible, for he cannot then get up and you will be able to think what to do next; otherwise he may spring up and carry on fighting. A truly panic-stricken horse will not listen to reason, and is terrifyingly strong

A yearling colt having fun pretending he's being chased. He turns his head to watch his heels, and raises his tail and feet high. A pony that had really been startled from behind would look like this, but his movements would be stiffer

pony so that she can see there is nothing to be bothered about. This is the natural way for ponies to learn, even when you are teaching them unnatural things. It is also important that you are calm and relaxed.

Fun. A pony that's happily excited moves in a quite different way. He prances, skips and leaps freely; often he twists or shakes his head and neck, quite unlike the stiff-necked frightened pony. He may play at being scared of something at his heels, tipping his nose high and to one side so he can see behind himself. He leaps forward with huge exaggerated steps and curls his tail over his back like a Pekinese; but his movements are springy rather than jerky, and his bounding run is completely different to the flat gallop of the real runaway. Other ponies have no difficulty in telling the

This pony is playing at bucking off a lion that's dropped out of the sky on to his back. Most of the moves that ponies play at are ones that might be useful in dangerous situations, like running away or getting rid of attackers. Sometimes they pretend that we are attackers, and have fun practising bucking us off. You can tell that this pony is only playing because his ears are forward; if he were frightened or angry they would be flat back.

Mostly, when ridden ponies buck they do it for fun, because they feel happy and well and safe. If you stay on, you can be sure that the pony wasn't really trying to get rid of you, although he may be trying to tell you that you or the saddle are making his back uncomfortable

difference between the two; they take no notice of the whirling maniac unless they want to join in the fun too.

Curiosity. Ponies are extremely inquisitive about anything strange. Pulled forward by their longing to investigate but pushed back by their fear, they hover about in an excited way, dithering forwards, backwards and round in circles, all attention on the oddity. While the tail and steps are high, the neck is arched, not straight and stiff as in a frightened pony. Sniffing, snorting, peering first with one eye then the other, the pony gradually persuades himself to get close enough to feel the object with his whiskers, nose and mouth. Once he knows what it smells like he is usually satisfied.

When your pony is curious, let him be. You can speed up the process by peering, sniffing and feeling the strange object yourself in a relaxed and cheerful way; but if you try to push him forward too fast his fear will only push him back again.

Pete and I were about to go swimming when he noticed this little girl and, inquisitive as ever, went to investigate. He stays at a safe distance where he can see her with both eyes, peering and sniffing. Another pony could tell from a long way off that he had seen something odd.

I have put my hands forward to leave his head free, but my reins are still short enough to stop him if he suddenly galloped off. He never wears a bit and is perfectly controllable in this bridle (Photo: Jane Turner)

This inquisitive pony is concentrating hard, his mouth tight and his nose long. He has forgotten about his back legs, which have ended up in strange positions. Sometimes a pony will walk forwards with his front feet but leave his back ones behind, so he stretches out like a rabbit. If he has no idea what a strange object is, he may bob his head up and down to change his focus on it and work out if it is small and near or large and far away

This mare, being startled, sprang straight into a trot from a standstill. When a horse makes an effort like this she has to shorten her back, and the sudden tightening of her muscles makes her tail lift and her head rise. Her mouth is tight and her nostrils flared as she peers behind her to see what has startled her

Movement.   The faster a pony moves, the more he shortens his back and the higher he carries his head and tail, until he reaches a flat-out gallop when his head drops again. When Pete sprints he sticks his tail straight up in the air so it floats behind him like a banner. It is actually the increase in speed, or wanting to go faster, that makes the head and tail rise. When you are trying to catch a difficult pony you can tell when he is about to rush off by this little rise of the head and tail, and if you slow down immediately he is not so likely to feel you are chasing him.

Meeting.   When a pony wants to meet another he raises his head, tail and feet, prancing forward in an eye-catching way.

Dullness.   When his head and tail are low the pony is in a calm or dull mood. Again you have to look at other signs to see whether he is merely relaxed or is miserable, feeling a bit off, or is sick or grumpy.

A relaxed pony moves in an easy, unhurried way. He moves his ears freely, pricking them at a sound or click of the fingers and turning to see any excitement. A dozy pony's mouth is so relaxed

Chalky has mild colic. His eyes and ears show that he's not much interested in anything else. His nostrils are slightly flared from the pain, his head is hanging, and his mouth is looser than if he were just grumpy it often droops open. When my old work-horse Tess was asleep on her feet her lower lip drooped so far that children would sneak up and post little bits of carrot or nuts into this letter-box, until she woke up with a start to find she had a surprise mouthful.

A sick pony looks at first sight merely dozy until you try to wake her up, when you realise that she has withdrawn, sunk into her misery. When you touch her her skin feels dead, like leather. Her eyes are dull, and her ears pay little attention, often flopping out sideways. Some kinds of sickness are painful, others not, and pain has its own signs; but sick ponies get dreadfully depressed. In the wild they would be the first for the wolves to take, and they behave as if they feel they have been condemned to death. Except in colic and laminitis, a sick pony usually refuses to lie down, fearing that he cannot get up again fast enough.

A sick pony often looks slightly scared, like this one. Her mouth is slack, though, and her ears and eyes do not seem to want to take anything in. Her nostrils are flared, for her breathing is faster than normal, and she has a slight tuck in her belly, a line that appears at the end of each breath. She would like to kick away the pain. A horse with mild colic, or a mare beginning to foal, shows these sorts of signs. A pony with laminitis has the same sort of face, but leans back to try to take the weight off her front feet, which are hot and painful.

There are many kinds of sickness but sick ponies always seem to be behaving strangely if you know them well

A dozy pony looks relaxed and dull. His head is low and his mouth droops. He rests one leg; the bones in the other one lock together so he doesn't fall over even when he is asleep. Ponies can't sleep soundly unless they lie down, but many ponies don't like you near them when they are lying down

A grumpy pony's body says 'Don't look at me', for his outline is dull. He is not resting his back leg but threatening to kick with it. He whisks his tail to try to get rid of irritation, wrinkles his nose and lays his ears back.

When a pony looks as bad-tempered as this, ask yourself why. If it is just that you have chosen to ride him when he'd prefer a nap, then groom him to please him and wake him up. If he usually looks like this there is something seriously wrong with his life or the way you ride him

Taffy is grumpy because someone threw a squib at him on Guy Fawkes' night and he panicked and cut his foot. He is not in pain any more but he is thoroughly fed up with being kept inside. He is normally sweet to Hannah.
  Compare this picture with the one of Chalky (p. 63). Taffy's ears are turned further back in temper, his eye is looking at Hannah, his nostril isn't flared and his mouth is quite tight (Photo: Jane Turner)

If your pony is affectionate and has a close relationship with you he will feebly ask for your attention and care when he feels ill. A big gentle gelding in a class I was teaching came up to me sighing to rest his head on me; but it wasn't until he'd done it several times (I didn't know him well) that I realised he had mild sand-colic. Less affectionate ponies do not want to be bothered by you when they are sick, and behave grumpily, wrinkling up their noses at the sight of you.

There are other reasons for grumpiness, too: being cold or tired; hating what you are about to do; not feeling in the mood for it; being unhappy from loneliness or miserable living conditions.

Cringing.   When a pony is utterly terrified by what is going on around her and can see no way out, she tries to make herself as small as possible, cringing, bending at the knees and tucking her tail under her. You see this often at horse sales, and when a big

This young mustang, being roped for the first time, is cringing in terror. Her neck and tail are stiff and she is mouthing, trying to stop the others from attacking her. This is a horrible way to treat any animal, especially the first time it sees humans. The roping horse, who is wise and steady, is watching the youngster over his shoulder and pulling on the rope. The second horse is watching the rope that his rider is whirling to catch the mustang's heels.

Like sheepdogs, these working cowponies really understand their job and will keep the rope steady and tight even when their riders jump off to catch the mustang or cow

A young pony that is afraid of an older pony, a person or another animal, will make herself as small as possible, tuck her tail under her, and mouth to beg not to be attacked. She keeps her ears well out of the way of trouble

bully goes for a young horse in a field. It is as if the pony is trying to hide inside her own skin, saying to other ponies 'I don't exist.'

I once rode a young racehorse that literally cringed herself off her feet. We were going up a narrow, high-banked Devonshire lane and met a man driving a pig. The filly was terrified, but I wouldn't let her turn and run. As the pig, a perfectly charming and friendly creature, waddled towards us the filly cringed and shook, shrinking herself down until I found my feet were on the ground. I got off and sat on the filly's neck to stop her from getting up; the pig and her owner went past; I urged the filly to her feet, got on again and we continued our morning exercise none the worse for wear.

Our outlines.   Because ponies look at outlines so carefully, they get startled or even scared when we change our outlines. If you carry an umbrella or wear a strange big hat, or even carry a bale of hay on your shoulders, you look quite different to them. Here in the mountains I often meet people carrying big rucksacks that come right above their heads so you cannot see they have any neck or head at all. Young ponies are almost always terrified of these strange new creatures until I can persuade the people to speak, which often isn't easy.

My ponies, which were quite used to the wild sights and sounds of local carnivals in which they appeared, were once almost stampeded by a man wearing one of those huge papier-mâché carnival heads. (Another time they were horrified was when a two-man 'camel', which they'd taken hardly any notice of, lifted its leg at a lamp-post and apparently peed like a dog. The hind-legs man was squeezing water from a squeezy bottle, but for some reason it was too much for their nerves.)

It is said that Bucephalus, Alexander the Great's horse, could not at first be ridden, for although he was quite tame, he panicked when he was mounted. Alexander, though only a boy, realised that the horse was afraid of his own shadow and rode him only towards the sun until he had calmed down. When I was a child this story seemed nonsense, for surely no horse is afraid of his own shadow; but then I realised that it was the strange outline of both horse *and* rider that so terrified Bucephalus.

Ears

You can tell a lot from a pony's ears, for they show what he is interested in. A healthy, lively pony has lively ears: they swivel round to concentrate on any sound he picks up. A depressed pony's ears are stiller; many riding-school ponies are so fed up with life that they stand with their ears out sideways, pointing to the ground, for they prefer to ignore the interesting sounds going on around them. Sick ponies often hold their ears sideways, too.

Ears pricked right forward mean that the pony is concentrating on what is in front of her. This may be because she likes the look of it, fears it or even hates it. I was once given a desperate pony that had been terribly beaten. She would canter straight up to you in the field, ears pricked, then turn and wallop you with both back feet. It took everybody by surprise since they thought that her pricked ears meant that she was friendly (which, eventually, she was, after I'd persuaded her that she wasn't going to have any more beatings). Most ponies, though, come to you only if they want to be with you, and they prick their ears because they are interested in a pleasant sort of way.

Watch your pony's ears on a ride. They flicker to and fro, from you to what is in front or to the blackbird in the hedge. The leading pony usually has his ears forward, while the followers hold theirs sideways or concentrate on their riders. This means that as a group the ponies have everything covered. As you overtake the leader your pony's ears go forward while his drop back.

When a pony's ears go back he is concentrating on what is behind. A pony trying to back out of something puts his ears back, to check if there is anything behind him. You see this when a pony is backing away from you or does not like what is in front of him. A ridden pony puts his ears back whenever you ask something difficult, not because he wants to back out but because he is concentrating on you.

Flattened ears mean the pony thinks he is in for trouble. It may be trouble that he is about to make, like attacking another pony or you, or it may be that he thinks you or another pony are about to attack him. It is always a warning sign, since ponies are quicker to spot trouble than we are, and of course they know when they are about to cause it.

The exact way a pony moves his ears also shows how he is feeling. A terrified pony may freeze like a rabbit so you can't really see anything is wrong; but his ears move much more quickly and jerkily than usual. When I am choosing a pony to buy I take particular notice of the way he holds and moves his ears. I like a pony that concentrates on what is going on, pointing his ears at anything new, for he is a bold, alert character. A pony whose ears tend to be checking nervously behind her doesn't have this zest for life; she tends to want to back out of new things rather than enjoying them.

Eyes

Ponies show the whites of their eyes when they roll them, or when they open their eyes wide because they are surprised or alert. It is said that you cannot trust a pony if he shows the whites of his eyes, but this is not always true. A pony may be very alert because he is anxious or nervous, when he is likely to be jumpy and untrustworthy. But he may also be a wide-awake character, like my wonderful piebald pony Mangas, who always showed the whites of his eyes but was splendidly bold and honest.

When a pony is concentrating on what is behind him but cannot turn his head he rolls his eyes as well as his ears backwards, so again you can see the whites. He may be frightened by what is behind him, or want to see that the way is clear for him to go backwards. It does not necessarily mean that he is bad-tempered, but it may do: a horse that is about to kick generally rolls his eyes back so he can see to aim properly.

Ponies can also roll their eyes forward when they are concentrating; some of them get an anxious little frown when they do this.

Face

Ponies make lots of different expressions with their faces. Some of them are quite deliberate signals, like showing the teeth as a warning that a bite will follow if you don't watch out. Others, like a saggy lip, probably aren't meant as signals, though you can tell what the pony is feeling from them.

A tight mouth means the pony is tense. Sometimes his whole chin dimples into a hard little lump. When he is tense and fearful a pony won't open his mouth. After his fear has passed he often makes little munching movements, loosening up again, and his head and neck move freely at the same time. You can take these as signs that he has relaxed and is ready to listen to you.

Some ponies get tense when you take off the bridle, so they can't let go of the bit. Instead, they jerk their heads up and hurt themselves by hanging on to the bit. This is what is called a self-fulfilling prophecy: that is, you think something is going to hurt so you tense up, which makes sure it does hurt. People who are afraid of having injections tense up their muscles so the needle does hurt, but if you relax as the needle goes in it doesn't hurt (much). If you have a pony that hangs on to the bit, get her to relax by cuddling her head, rubbing her nose and opening her mouth gently with your thumb as you take off the bridle. If you manage to do this a few times

Shakertown, a Morgan stallion. His long nose shows that he is interested and wanting something; his tight mouth and chin show that he is tense; his pricked ears and eyes are concentrating madly on what is in front of him. It's a mare going past.

A horse with a mouth as tight as this could not accept a titbit nor let go of his bit without the pony getting hurt, she will lose her fear, relax her mouth by herself, and let the bit drop.

A saggy mouth means the pony is completely relaxed and dozy.

A long nose shows that the pony is interested and concentrating. If he is worried he will have a tight mouth. If he is trying to work out what is in front of him he will probably have flared nostrils too, since he will be trying to smell at the same time. If he is playful, or wanting food or other sorts of attention, his mouth and neck will not be stiff and tight although his nose is long, and his movements will show what he wants.

You will also see a long nose when a pony is scratching his withers or rump on a branch or post, when his nose stretches and wiggles in pleasure. When ponies want to groom their friends by scratching each other's withers they saunter up in a relaxed way, their noses long and searching, and their mouths slightly open. Your pony may make this face at you when he wants to be groomed.

Flehmen, the rolled-back nose (see p.44–45), shows that the pony is trying to taste or smell something odd. Stallions do it particularly when they smell an in-season mare; some geldings do, too. Emma, my big, gentle, half-Arab mare, twice did it not because of any odd smell but because something very odd happened. Once she was galloping across the sand, shook her head hard and her bridle fell off; the other time a beginner fell off her in a most peculiar way. Both times Emma immediately stopped, stuck her nose in the air and did *Flehmen*. It was her own personal way of saying that she thought the situation was weird.

When they are in pain, especially in sharp belly-pain as in colic or foaling, ponies may roll back the top lip in a way that looks a bit like *Flehmen*; but in this case they don't take a deep breath and throw their heads in the air, and the movement is quicker and less strong.

Yawning usually means that the pony is bored and tired, as it does with us. But a pony that often yawns during or after eating is trying to clean lumps of food off his teeth. This probably means he has sharp teeth, so he should have his teeth checked and rasped.

When a pony is annoyed by you, other ponies, pain, or whatever is going on, she wrinkles her nostrils. You can usually work out what is annoying her; lots of ponies do it when the girth is done up, especially when it is done roughly. Pete, who is sensitive and expressive, wrinkles his nose whenever you do something in a way he doesn't like. If, for instance, he doesn't like the way you're brushing him he wrinkles his nose. He thinks you will understand that and mend your ways, but if you don't he shows his annoyance

Lulu, a thoroughbred mare, has ticklish flanks and when her rider puts her feet too far back Lulu is furious. She wrinkles her nose in disgust, puts her ears back, lashes her tail and threatens to kick. If you are riding a horse that gets as angry as this, change what you are doing before getting annoyed yourself in a different way, by flicking his tail. If you still don't take any notice he loses his temper and snaps at you, because he has run out of polite ways of trying to stop you.

Flared nostrils mean that the pony is smelling something ahead (ears will be forward) or that she is panting from exercise, pain or fear. When ponies are in bad pain the whole body shape usually says that they are depressed; the ears are relaxed; the mouth is relaxed; the eyes are dull and unseeing; but the nostrils are flared, as if they were excited or lively. People in bad pain often show the same signs. In colic, though, sudden sharp stabbing pains make the pony much more agitated: she will lash her tail, look at her sides as if she can't understand why they should hurt, paw, stamp, and roll wildly. Again her nostrils will be flared as she pants from pain.

Some high-spirited ponies flap the lower lip when they are excited but controlled, for instance when starting exercise before they have settled properly, or during travelling in a trailer.

Ponies show their teeth as a clear sign that they are about to bite, or feel like biting.

Mouthing or jawing is a funny snapping movement that foals and yearlings do to older horses, especially strange ones; it's a bit like puppies rolling on their backs when they meet older dogs. The foal stretches out his head, cringes, opens his mouth wide with the lips drawn back so you can see his teeth, and moves his jaws as if he were trying to bite something too big for his mouth. It's a way of saying: 'Don't bite me, I'm only little.' Foals do it to all horses – a new-born foal may do it to you, too, or a cow, or a wheelbarrow – but as they get older and stronger they do it only to horses they think may attack them.

Tails

Tails are brilliant signallers, for they change the pony's outline so that they're easily noticed. Ponies carry their tails high when they are excited, raised when they are moving, low when they are relaxed and flat when they are frightened. Sometimes a terrified pony puts his tail right between his legs and scares himself (for by that time he is goofy with fear) into thinking there is a snake wrapped round his hocks. Recently I saw a two-year-old colt at a sale who was so petrified that he kept kicking out at his own tail, which he'd tucked under his belly. I've also seen people bucked off young horses that were really too frightened to be ridden, for the same reason. If you're riding a pony that's scared from behind you can feel his tail tuck under him as he leaps forward.

Young colt mouthing at an older pony. When he pulls his lips back you can see the white and pink of his teeth and tongue, so it is an obvious signal to other horses. But he is not as frightened as the mustang yearling: he is being polite.

Both these ponies are watching me as well as each other

Mares also raise their tails when they are in season (that is, ready to be mated) and they think there is a stallion about. It is a clear signal to the stallion. The mare stands quite still, back humped, without all the other signs that might show she is raising her tail because she's been startled. She then produces a strong-smelling pee and 'winks' her back end so you (and the stallion) can see a quick flash of pink, another eye-catching sign. Try to notice when your mare comes in season; it happens for about five days every three weeks during spring and summer, but most mares show strongly only for the last two days. Some mares, often young ones that have not had a foal, get silly when they are in season, behaving ridiculously with other horses or barging you about. If your mare behaves strangely every now and then, keep a diary of it and you may find that it happens when she is in season. If you go to a show with an in-season mare you must keep well clear of stallions, for she will try to get to them and will cause a rumpus if she does.

Tail-lashing or whisking is the way that horses get rid of annoying flies. They also use it to mean they are annoyed by anything else: you, other ponies, pain or the saddle, for instance. Work out which! A ridden pony lashes his tail when he is annoyed by the rider: when he is asked to do something difficult, when the rider is rough or careless, or when he doesn't want to do what he is asked. A very angry pony lashes her tail furiously, especially when she is about to bite or attack.

A ridden pony that is tense holds his tail stiffly, sometimes sticking it straight out behind him even at a trot. When you are watching dressage, for instance, notice which horses hold their tails stiffly; these ones are not relaxed and comfortable with what they are doing. A happy horse lets his tail swing freely at slow paces.

When they are nervous, ponies dung a lot, even to the point of getting diarrhoea. They may also lift their tails as if they were about to dung but without doing anything. You see this particularly when a pony is being urged forward towards something that frightens him.

Movements

Ponies are particularly sensitive to movement, and they use movements as signals.

Head movements.   When a pony is attacked from in front he jerks his head back and up, tensing his neck suddenly. He also does a head-jerk if he thinks he's being threatened, or is being pushed forward into something he finds threatening. You often see a head-jerk when a pony is refusing to cross a ditch, for instance. A pony that has been hit about the head will do a head-jerk whenever you raise an arm suddenly in front of him. Unfortunately, if you are holding him by the bridle he will hit himself in the mouth with the bit, which will only prove to him that arms are dangerous, painful things when they move fast. Take care not to wave your arms about excitedly in front of your pony.

Ponies nudge us with their noses when they want attention. Ponies that have been fed too many titbits nudge your pockets, but others do it out of friendliness (they do it to each other, too), because they want to be groomed or fed, or want your attention in some other way. Pete often nudges my shoulder when I am walking with him, or my knee when I am riding him, when something interesting has caught his attention and he wants to know what I think of it. Once I was riding him up an overgrown track in the

Head bob: When a pony stares at something, with his ears pricked, and bobs his head up and down, he is trying to work out how far away and how big the thing is

Jerk back: When a pony is afraid of being hit on the head he jerks his head back

Nudge: Ponies nudge us, or their friends, to get attention

Head thrust: When a pony jerks his head up and forward, with his ears flat back, he is deliberately signalling that he is annoyed and may attack

Shake: Ponies shake their heads to get rid of flies, but they also do it when they are irritated by the bit, the bridle, the reins being too tight, or being bothered for instance by being shut up too long. They toss their heads up and down for the same reasons

Swing: Ponies swing their heads to one side to avoid being hit or, more slowly, to be able to see with one eye when they are too close to see with both eyes

Nose swing: Some ponies tuck their noses in and swing them from side to side when they are feeling brave, pleased and playful. Stallions do it when they are courting mares

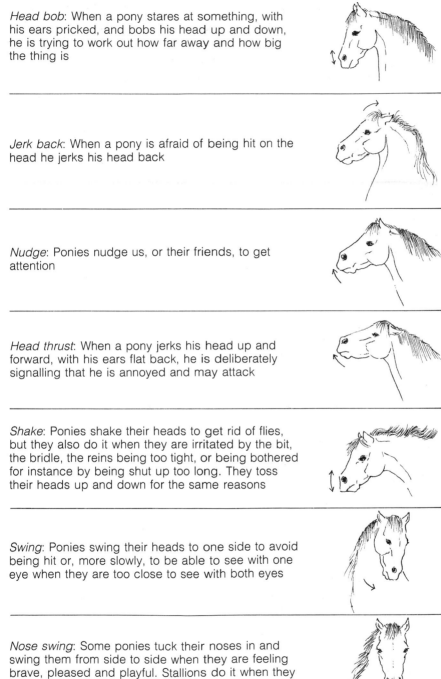

Forestry when he stopped, his foot apparently caught in brambles. Thinking he was being feeble about pulling it free, I urged him on; but he turned and nudged my knee, quite hard, and held his leg straight out in front of him for me to see. Round his lower leg was a wire snare set for deer. If he had not had the sense to call my attention to it, but had panicked as most ponies would have done, he'd have damaged his tendons for life.

A head-thrust, when the pony jerks her head forward suddenly or lunges forward with her head outstretched, is a threat: the pony is saying 'Get out of my space or I'll attack you.' You see it when ponies are squabbling over food, or a mare is driving another pony away from her foal. Many stabled horses do it when someone walks past their door.

Nodding, tossing or shaking the head are ways of getting rid of flies or irritation round the face. Ponies also use them to show that they are irritated by other things too. Some ponies shake or toss their heads when they are ridden. This may mean that the bit does not suit them, or that the rider is too heavy-handed for a light, sensitive mouth; if the pony changes when you change the bit, ride without a bit, or ride with a loose rein, you will know that you have found out what was bothering her. But in some ponies it is a long-standing habit that started years ago, when the pony had a rider who was rough with her mouth, or even when she was first broken in. However kindly it is done, being 'broken in' to ride is rather strange and unnatural, and many ponies start doing rather odd things to show they are bothered by it. If the trainer takes time and lets the pony relax, these funny habits disappear; but if he, or the next rider, goes on demanding too much of the pony the habit sets in, leaving you with the problem years later. Pete, for instance, couldn't stand wearing a browband for the first months he was ridden, though he's never been irritated by one since.

Neck-wringing is a peculiar twisting and tossing that some ponies, particularly Arabs, do when they are keyed up and are not sure what to do next. You see it when they are playing and they are going away from others; some ponies do it more out of irritation, like the head-shaking above.

When a stallion herds his mares he holds his head low and wobbles it from side to side in a strange snakey-necked way. When a mare sees a stallion rushing up to her in this odd way she knows immediately she is being herded. Some ponies do it when they are chasing dogs (my donkey is a great terroriser of dogs), though then the movement is not so snakey.

Occasionally a pony will bite your feet when you are riding. This is usually to get at horseflies, which tend to bite the thin skin behind the girth, and not to get at you at all; you should reach down and slap the fly since the pony can't reach it himself. It may be, though, that you are the 'fly' and you are irritating the pony by using your legs too roughly. A good squeeze urges the pony forward much better than a kick.

Leg movements. Some ponies, especially mares, strike out with one forefoot when they meet other ponies and touch noses. They usually squeal at the same time. This is not a real attack but it is a warning to the other pony not to come too close. If you have a mare like this, take care where you stand when she is meeting other ponies. A shod forefoot can hurt your knee badly, though if you stand to one side and make sure the ponies are meeting at right angles nobody will get hurt.

Pawing with a front foot is a sign of frustration. Like many other signals it does have a purpose in a pony's natural life, but it also comes to signal the sort of feeling that goes with that purpose. Ponies paw snow and ice in winter when they want to get at the grass and water beneath. Pawing then comes to mean 'I want to get at something but I can't.' Ponies paw when they are waiting for their food, and some greedy ones paw when they are eating it, as if they can't bear the time it takes to stuff it down themselves. If your pony does that, feed her in an earthenware sink or put her bucket in a car tyre; it's no use yelling at her to stop. Ponies paw the fence or a stable door when they want to get out, and you often see stallions at shows pawing furiously because they can't get at the mares parading past.

A gentler sort of pawing is done when the pony is about to roll. Preferring to roll in sand or dust, he loosens up the earth first. If you watch your pony you will see him wiggle his nose in the loose earth before he goes down; he's testing the smell and feel of the spot. When you are riding you can tell when a pony is about to roll because he drops his head to smell, paws gently, and sags at the knees going down. Getting his head up and pushing him on stops him rolling, but when we go to the beach my ponies so adore rolling in the soft sand that they go straight down like ninepins, for they are canny enough to know they'll be stopped if they give any warning.

Stamping gets rid of flies and itches on the pasterns and legs; some ponies also stamp their back legs when they are fed up with being tied up or standing too long in the stable. But if you have a pony with a lot of feather (hairy legs) and he stamps a good deal, feel through the feather in his back pastern and heel. Such ponies get 'grease' which forms irritating sores there. They can be treated by clipping the feather and using soothing cream.

Ponies kick at flies on their bellies, and they may also kick at you if you are using the wrong brush or touch there. The skin under the belly is particularly sensitive. There is a big whorl of hair, with a bare patch in the middle, under a pony's belly, and when he lies with his legs under him to sleep this bare patch can get rubbed raw. Flies, especially the tiny, maddening ones, work to open a sore here, so if your pony seems particularly irritated by being brushed here, have a look to see he is not bleeding.

Defence and attack

When a pony wants to defend himself, particularly against attack from behind, he kicks. If you suddenly run behind a pony, especially when he is tied up, he is likely to lash out without warning because you have startled him and he cannot see what or who you are. But if you corner him and he wants to get rid of you he warns you first. His first warning is to turn his rump on you in a definite way, watching you over his shoulder with one eye. This means that if you go on 'attacking' he may kick. If you then stop, relax and wait for him to relax you will get him out of the feeling that he's being attacked and into the feeling that it's only little old you and he might as well be friendly. If you push on too fast he may warn you again by showing you one back foot or even waving it at you. Black Jack, a sweet-natured cob, hated the hens and dogs trying to steal the food from his bucket and would warn them most politely that his back feet could hurt, but they never understood his meaning.

Most ponies don't kick unless they feel they have been forced to; but if they find that a back-end threat sends you scurrying away they may come to use that as an easy way of getting rid of you.

If (heaven forbid) you find yourself shut in a stable with a vicious horse and he corners you and is clearly about to kick, your best defence is not to cower in the corner but to leap forward as noisily as you can. This will make him jump forward and turn to face you.

Ponies attack head-on, by charging and biting. Again they try to avoid really fighting by warning. The first warning is flattened ears. Head-thrusts, tail-lashing and showing the teeth give stronger warnings. If none of these works the pony lunges forward and bites. You see these sorts of attack at feeding times, when bossy ponies attack others.

Very few ponies attack us in this way, luckily; it is not in their nature to do it, and a pony has to be treated badly over quite a long time before he gets that angry. Mostly when they bite us they do it much more sneakily, with a nip rather than a bite. There is much less warning then, but if your pony is the nippy sort watch out for the irritated wrinkled nose that tells you he is in a bad mood.

Extremely vicious or angry ponies sometimes attack with the front legs, trying to knock each other off their feet. Stallions fight like this; mares usually turn round and kick each other. Oddly enough, wild stallions are not nearly as dangerous to each other as tame ones are. In the wild, stallions usually have plenty of room to avoid each other; when they meet they try to scare each other off by snorting, prancing around and dunging on each other's dung (like dogs taking turns peeing on car wheels), and serious fights happen only when one stallion, usually a young one, is trying to steal another one's mares. Tame stallions are often kept alone, which makes them keyed up since they naturally feel they should own a few mares; and because they don't live in a group they don't get clever at using body language and threats, so they end up fighting more often if they are given the chance. It is the way stallions are kept that makes them dangerous.

Some colts and stallions, and occasionally mares with young foals, attack small animals like snakes, dogs and lambs, pouncing on them with their front feet. I have seen two large rattlesnakes literally shredded by a penned colt in Arizona. He probably would have run away if he'd had the chance.

When a pony attacks another, he charges forward with his head outstretched, his ears flat back, his teeth showing and his tail lashing. Usually this is quite enough to scare off the other pony without there being a real fight

Signs that a pony feels cooped up

As we have seen, ponies living naturally don't get themselves into tight corners. Being stabled all day, especially when they cannot touch or play with their friends, puts a lot of strain on them. They don't like being inside: they have nothing to do; they are lonely; and since they get fed on concentrated food they don't spend eight or nine hours a day wiggling their noses about and munching on the hundred different plants they usually have to sort through. They are like fish out of water.

Many stabled ponies start to do strange things that soon become habits. Some of these arise from the movements they make when they are irritated, like head shaking or nodding; sometimes they are signs of anger, like head-thrusts or biting. Sometimes they show the need to use their mouths more by chewing the woodwork, or by sticking out their tongues and holding them between their teeth. Sometimes it's the need to move, to feel free, that comes out in stall-walking or pawing and banging at the door.

If you watch carefully when you visit stables where the horses are kept inside almost all the time you will see these and other movements of the same sort, usually done again and again and again as if by a machine. Often the people who look after these horses say, 'Oh, it's just his funny habit,' or shout at the horse to stop. But these signals are urgent messages that the horse is not happy being cooped up.

Many of these habits seem fairly harmless, and people ignore the horses' cries for freedom. But there are other habits which are taken more seriously because they stop the horse from eating or being in tip-top condition. These are called 'stable vices'; the most common are weaving, crib-biting and wind-sucking. In weaving the horse stands with his head over the door and rocks from side to side, swinging his head. In crib-biting he takes the top of the manger or door (or anything else the right height) in his teeth and sucks in air with a funny gulping sound. In wind-sucking he does the same without holding on to anything, arching his neck and tightening his muscles.

Horses with bad stable vices lose weight; cribbers and wind-suckers change the shape of their necks, too, so none of them wins prizes. That is why stable vices are thought to be important, while other habits aren't. It seems terrible that we people are so selfish that we take no notice of a horse's misery until it gets in the way of our pleasure or our ambition. The most horrible habit I have seen was in an extremely valuable Arab stallion who bit his own

Chalky windsucking. He arches his neck, pulls his nose in and swallows air. Chalky is an ex-showjumper. Being kept in too much and competed too hard made him start this awful habit, which is a kind of self-hypnosis. He finally did it so much that he was useless. However he is now in a riding school where he has friends, freedom and varied work, so he is much happier. Now he only windsucks when he is miserable, which in this case is because he had colic and was shut in sides as if maddened by flies. 'He can't go out,' I was told, 'he might hurt himself.' The horse's sides were raw, bloody messes.

You can force some horses to stop their habits with mechanical devices, but they often start doing something even worse, for you have done nothing to stop their misery. The only way you can change that is to turn them out and keep them as they want. But if you do have to keep your pony inside there is a lot you can do to stop him getting so miserable in the first place. You can keep a friend in the same box with him. You may have to tie them while they are fed their concentrates, but the rest of the time they will get on fine and amuse each other. If your boxes are too small to keep more than one pony in, knock a hole in the wall so neighbours can reach and muzzle each other. If there isn't another pony, keep a donkey, goat or sheep in the box. Give the ponies all your vegetable waste except sprouting potatoes (poisonous). They won't like onion skins but it will keep them busy sorting them out. Whole turnips or beet, or branches of gorse, keep them busy, too. If your pony likes to fiddle with things, give him something to play with, like a knotted rope or things hung from the ceiling. Let him listen to a radio. If you learn to use your eyes and see the signs of unhappiness that many stabled horses show you will realise that these things are not silly. They mean far more to the pony than being clean, or having his rosettes pinned up, or his name over the door, or any more of the nonsense that people get up to. If you enjoy your pony, the least you can do is to make sure he's not being driven slowly mad with unhappiness.

Sweats and shivers

Ponies sweat when they are hot from galloping about, of course, but sweating can also be a sign of fear, excitement or pain. Ponies that are frightened by being shut up alone or travelling in a trailer sweat from sheer terror, and if your pony does this you might think of some way of sparing her by arranging company for her. Excited ponies sweat, too; when I'm riding Max bareback and he sees a mare I can feel a great flush of heat come from him straight away. Ponies in pain sweat patchily, often on the face, and as they are neither excited nor hot this adds to the queer combination of signals they are giving.

Like sweating, shivering or trembling can be a sign of temperature, in this case cold, but it can also mean fear, excitement or shock. Really frightened ponies that cannot run away from what frightens them tremble or shudder, as we do when we are terrified.

This is a far kinder way of keeping horses than locking them up by themselves. They have plenty of space and can nuzzle and play with each other. Their haynets are hung high on the ropes behind and they have fun swinging them around. The water barrel is fed from a stream and has an overflow so they always have fresh water. The deep litter bed is surprisingly warm and they are rugged in cold weather. You can keep three horses or five ponies in this barn, and even without much exercise they keep well, happy, and never start stable vices

Shock after an accident makes them shake too. Ponies suffer more from shock than is often realised, and they need nursing for it in the same way as we do, with warmth, quiet comfort and company.

Skin-wriggling is another way of getting rid of flies. It is also a sign of sore or irritated skin. If your pony wriggles the skin on his back when you stroke him, the saddle may be rubbing. By feeling gently you can usually find a hot spot that is the cause of the trouble. Max used to wriggle his skin terribly when I first rode him and wanted him to go the opposite way to where he wanted. It was his way of saying:'You're just a great big *fly* that's bothering me; I wish you'd buzz off and leave me alone.'

The Steed always turns to touch Richard when he is near her, not because he feeds her titbits but because she is fond of him

Body chess

If you watch ponies loose in a field together you will see that they are constantly playing a sort of game, moving themselves around like chess pieces to block, threaten or encourage each other. By standing sideways a pony can block another pony's way forward. Mangas, my mad old piebald, hated to be caught and would try to block the other ponies from getting to us in ways that were quite funny to watch. Mares with new foals often use their bodies to shield their precious babies, blocking us from getting to them, and a jealous mare will block her stallion from getting to any other mares in the group.

Ponies when playing will head each other off at the gallop, or even use a shoulder-barge to shove another pony out of the way. Polo ponies are encouraged to 'ride off' other ponies with a shoulder-barge when they are both heading for the same ball.

Although she enjoys being stroked and rubbed, it must be in the right way or she gets annoyed

Galloping up a narrow track a pony that doesn't want to be overtaken will try to block an overtaker, who will then use a shoulder-barge or head off the other pony so he is forced to slow down.

A mare guarding her sleeping foal stands facing any danger or threat, showing that she will defend her foal if necessary. Recently, camping with a friend who was on a six-month ride, I noticed that all night long his mare, who adores him (the feeling is mutual), stood guard over him so that Pete could not get anywhere near him.

By galloping past from behind, a pony can startle another pony, encouraging her to be swept up to follow him and join his game. By walking past, a bully can make another pony run away, for the power of her temper spreads like a cloud round her. When we are riding in a group, ponies go on playing these games to move each other about unbeknown to us, and you may find your pony doing things that were asked for not by you but by another pony. It is difficult to work out what is going on when you are riding but by watching ponies playing together you can understand the moves better.

When they are scared, ponies bunch together, touching shoulders. Ponies sometimes do this when we are leading them, too. They are not trying to knock us down but are crowding up for reassurance, wanting, so to speak, to have their hands held. Your best reply to this is not to knock the pony away angrily, which makes him feel even more scared and lost, but to put your hand firmly on his neck, walking on and showing him that you have no fear yourself. As time goes on you will find that he feels safer every time you put your hand on his neck, even when riding, and that this becomes part of the language you share together.

Ponies that are friends stay close together in a field, often facing the same way, touching and rubbing against each other and resting together, flicking the flies off each other's faces. Friendly ponies touch us and rub us in the same way. Just as a mare turns to touch her foal when she is suckling, a pony will turn to touch the blacksmith's back as he bends to shoe her, or to touch us as we do up the girth. It is their way of making sure who we are.

Voice

Ponies use their voices a good deal. Some of their calls, like neighs, nickers and squeals, are usually given to other ponies; others, like sighs, groans and nose-blowing, aren't. But calls don't seem to have exact meanings like words do, for different ponies give them in different situations, just as some dogs bark when there's someone at the door, for food, when they want to go out and when they are excited, while other dogs hardly ever bark.

Ponies' voices differ just as ours do; they obviously recognise each other's voices, and ours.

Neigh (whinny). Every pony has his own special neigh, and can recognise his friends' neighs. Some are musical, sounding like a peal of bells, while others sound more like roars. Stallions do an extra little grunting bit on the end of the neigh, so you can tell a stallion is coming long before you see him. This is handy for you and other ponies to know.

A neigh can mean several things. It's a call that ponies make when they are separated from others, when they see or hear others in the distance suddenly, or when they recognise a friend's voice or footsteps. It can mean 'Anyone there?' or 'Hi, who are you?'

Seren threatens Dane with a head-thrust (which he doesn't understand) because he has come between her and Jane. Horses don't only play body chess with each other: the places that we or dogs stand have exact meanings to them too

or 'Hello, so-and-so, it's me' or 'Come back.' It can show worry, as it does when a pony is suddenly separated from his friends and shut up alone; pleasure, as when friends meet; challenge, as it did when old Maestoso neighed every morning when he came out of the stable into his field. But it is usually a long-distance call; it says who the giver is, and asks anyone else around to say who they are.

Ponies use their neighs in different ways. Max, Maestoso's son, neighs in reply when I call to him and he can't see me, but he doesn't come up to me; it's up to me to find him. Pete, though, doesn't neigh but arrives silently. Pete hardly ever neighs except when he is in trouble, lonely or worried, for instance when he wants his tether moved, or when he's in a trailer and I call back to him from the front; he uses a special high-pitched neigh that sounds like a foal taken from his mother. Perhaps that's because at those times he's calling to me as if I were his mother, for comfort. He and Max are good friends, but he rarely neighs when they see each other after being parted; Max does. Max, though, has never neighed to me for help, though he sometimes neighs when he's startled while dozing, out of sheer surprise. Both of them clearly know that my high-pitched whoop and the donkey's bray (they both love her) are peculiar kinds of neigh. The only way you can learn exactly when and why your pony neighs is by watching and listening. Most people learn what their own pony means without really thinking about it, and then are put out when another pony doesn't mean the same thing. If Pete neighed when I went past I'd go and see what was the matter with him; if Max did I'd just shout 'Hi!' back and go on my way.

Nickering   is a softer, lower call that's usually given when ponies are near to each other and want to be nearer still: 'Come closer, friend.' Three common sorts of nicker, which all sound different, are the gentler nicker of a mare calling her foal to her, the powerful, seductive nicker of a stallion fancying a mare, and the 'Please, please' nicker of your pony when you arrive with his food. Again you will find that some ponies nicker more than others. I don't think this means they like you more, merely that they are more talkative. Some ponies nicker pathetically as if they're weak with hunger, and others don't make a sound, though you can see their nostrils moving. Max only nickers to mares; when he wants food he does a special high neigh.

Squeals   are usually given when ponies are very close to each other and are not quite sure whether they want to be. When ponies meet and are sniffing noses a squeal often comes before a foreleg strike. Mares and fillies squeal more than stallions and geldings; they squeal most when they are just coming into season and are flirting without being ready to mate. When you meet a youngster who sniffs your face as if you were another pony, if you squeal suddenly he will jump back, so squeals seem to mean 'Watch out and mind your manners.'

Some ponies also squeal when they are in a real temper and are about to kick or bite another pony. A hot-tempered mare I rebroke after she had been roughly broken by cowboys (actually she broke most of them) used to squeal whenever she was about to go off in a bucking fit, which was handy as I could quickly ask her to do something else.

Squeals are often heard when ponies are playing wildly and nipping each other.

Screams and roars   are usually heard during real fights and attacks. Stallions scream and roar much more than mares; they may roar even when just seeing another horse. There is usually a good deal of rage, fear and excitement going on.

Snorts are alarm calls, given when the horse is startled. A good snort carries a long way. Once I was sent a little mare who was silly about pigs, so I put her on the hill where two pigs roamed free. When she met them I could hear the snorts right up the mountain, three miles away. Unfortunately the pigs never understood her meaning, which was definitely 'Go away!' Stallions, being the guardians of a group, snort more than mares; they do it in alarm and challenge at other stallions, surprises, tigers and stray horrors like pigs. If you are near a pony that snorts loudly you will realise the noise makes him sound huge and dragonish, which is obviously the point. When one of their group snorts, other ponies clearly understand there is danger about.

Ponies also snort when they are playing at shooing off tigers. If you want your pony to raise his tail and feet and prance as he does when alarmed, blowing loudly and suddenly will encourage him. You can have very good games in a small arena like this.

Mix-ups. When ponies are excited and agitated, for instance when good friends are parted in a strange place, they often make calls that are mix-ups between neighs, nose-blowing and various other sounds.

Groans aren't directed at other ponies. They are given by sick ponies, or those in pain, much like our groans.

Grunts are given mostly when the horse is making a great effort. Pete does a half-grunt, half-squeal when he is indignant about having his rug adjusted roughly, or is kicked by a rude rider.

Sighs. Ponies, like us, sigh when they are fed up, bored or a bit annoyed. They also sigh, as we do, with relief after being tense. Many ponies hold their breath when they are tense, only letting it go when the problem has passed, so a sigh may come at the same time as other signs of relaxing: small munching movements, sudden freedom of head and neck, and shifting the feet.

Nose-blowing gets rid of tickles round the nose and whiskers. Ponies also blow their noses when they are strolling home after a good ride, perhaps because the exercise makes their noses run a bit. At that time it's a comfortable sort of sound, and it often sets others off. You can sometimes get your pony to blow his nose by making the same kind of sound yourself at the right time. Ponies are great copy-cats.

High blowing is a noise that some high-spirited horses make when they are settling into work, especially cantering, a kind of 'hrrrrmph' that comes at every step. In these horses the skin that divides the two nostrils high up inside is flappy, and when they are blowing their breath out hard it vibrates. They do it when they are in a jolly mood.

Whistling and roaring are noises made by horses that have damaged vocal cords (voicebox) from being galloped too hard when unfit. A horse that whistles or roars cannot be passed as 'sound in wind' by a vet. This is not, of course, the same kind of roar as that made in anger.

Smells

Ponies send smell-messages to each other. This sounds strange to us, but many animals do it. Dung and pee can be used deliberately to show 'I am so-and-so and I went this way at such-and-such a time.' Stallions mark other horses' droppings with their own, to let other horses know they are in the area. Unfortunately we can't tell what messages have been left; the best we can do is to notice when our ponies are smelling something interesting and to see what they do about it.

Smell-messages are used particularly in mating. An in-season mare's pee has a special smell that attracts the stallion, and she instantly pees whenever she meets a strange horse, just in case he is a stallion. You can learn to recognise this smell yourself, but stallions are far more sensitive to it: stallions have made sexy noises at me when I've been wearing a coat that I'd worn when riding an in-season mare days before. Once Max and an in-season mare were ridden out together. After a while they parted, she to trot ahead down the road while he took a longer trail through the woods. After ten minutes he'd forgotten about her, but later when he crossed the road lower down he instantly started neighing and prancing about, though it was at least forty minutes since she'd passed that way and she had neither peed nor dunged; he must have been smelling her footsteps, or her wonderful perfume hanging in the air.

When you are riding a stallion it is obvious from his excitement whether he's smelled another horse, whether it's a mare, gelding or stallion, and whether a mare is in season. But all horses are just as sensitive to each other's smells, though they don't react so violently.

Max always smells the top of his gate to see whether the mares from the local riding school have passed this way recently

Your pony's language

Ponies, like us, are all individuals and like us they use their language slightly differently, especially when they are 'talking' to us. Young or wild ponies behave the same to us as they would to other ponies, for they know no other language. As time goes on they usually realise that we are foreigners who don't speak the same language unless we have made an effort to learn. Some of them, like riding-school ponies who are constantly surrounded by ignorant beginners, give up trying to communicate; others, more fortunate, work out special signs as they see that their owners react to them. Shakertown, a Morgan stallion I trained, was a stabled show horse. He loved to go out, and when he thought it was his turn he'd stand stock still with his head low and his nose growing longer and longer until it went off sideways. 'Shake's nose has gone squiffy again' they'd say, and everybody knew that I'd have to take him out or he'd lose his temper with anyone else who went in to him. After a while he realised that we were reacting to his signal and would twist his nose in what seemed to be a quite deliberate signal whenever I appeared.

Like us, ponies like to be understood. As you watch and think about your pony's language you will find he becomes happier and more willing, that even if your riding skill does not improve you become a better rider, and that you get on better together. You will also find that your pony understands much more about you and your body language than you have realised before.

Chapter 6

What you tell your pony

As well as understanding each other's signals, ponies are clever at understanding ours. Actually they are cleverer than we think, for they often see things that we don't realise we are saying.

You talk to your pony in several ways: with your voice, with the aids, and with body language. Mostly you mean to use the first two, but a lot of the time you don't realise what your body language is saying.

Voice

Ponies are as good as dogs at learning voice commands like whoa, walk, trot, pick it up (foot) and so on. Most of them aren't trained very well, though; if you want a pony to learn voice commands you must be sure to reward him when he does the right thing. They are good at understanding your tone of voice, too, and they take just as much notice of that as of the words you use. If you scream 'whoa' in a panic no pony will stop, for the tone of your voice is telling him to belt off as fast as possible, but even if he is in a panic a well-trained pony will stop and stand calmly if you manage to speak to him calmly.

Like body language, tone of voice is something that takes a good deal of practice to control. Try using really angry, scolding words in a loving tone, or the other way round, and you'll find it's confusing not only to the animals you speak to but also to yourself. It's impossible to sound convincing. You'll see that animals react more to your tone of voice than to the words. Try doing the same thing to your friends without any warning and see what they make of it.

You might get them to stand still by bellowing at them, but if you shriek furiously at them to relax and feel comfortable they won't be able to. To a frightened pony, the only way to stop wanting to escape is to relax and feel comfortable, and he can't do that if you yell at him.

As you will find, learning to keep your voice calm when you too are frightened by what is going on is difficult, and the only way to sound convincingly soothing is to learn to relax yourself even when World War III is breaking out. Tone of voice and body language go together.

The aids

The aids are deliberate body signals that ponies naturally understand. All a pony does when he responds to the aids is to move whichever bit of him you have put pressure on. He is simply trying to make himself more comfortable. When you press your leg against him he moves away from it; when you tighten a rein he moves his head so the rein goes loose again. People do exactly the same when you push or pull gently at them.

If you try steering a friend around with little pushes and pulls, you'll find that as long as you are gentle and your friend is not alarmed, he will do what you hope. But if you grab at him, or thump him, he'll do exactly the opposite instead. Try it the other way round; you'll behave the same. So does a pony.

Do remember this when you are riding.

If you use the aids properly but do not put a bit in the pony's mouth you can ride a calm pony that's never been ridden before, steering and stopping without any difficulty. If the pony is relaxed and ready he does not buck or run away; he moves about in a rather dreamy way, amazed and interested in this strange new game of being pushed about gently. If he is not ready but is fearful and tense he will not give to the pressure and allow himself to be guided; instead he will fight back. When we train a pony at a simple level all we do is to encourage him to relax so he is sensitive to the aids, and to praise and reward him for it. He doesn't have to learn anything special, unlike you. For you, the rider, it's much more difficult: you have to learn exactly where to do the pushing, and how to put it all together, as well as relaxing.

The pony does not, of course, know or care about the struggle you have had to learn how to use the aids. He responds to them as naturally as he does to your other body language, the stuff you don't realise you are saying. And just as it's confusing when you say something in the 'wrong' tone of voice, so it's confusing if your unconscious body language is giving signals that are different from the ones you think you are giving.

Misunderstandings.   The most obvious example of this is the nervous beginner whose pony decides she's had enough and is going home now. Scared, the rider does what every human being on earth does when scared unless he's specially learned not to: he goes stiff, crouching and leaning forward. This is pure instinct. Anyone in danger hunches up to protect his soft stomach and his heart. As he does this his arms and legs stiffen and fold up slightly; his shoulders hunch; his whole body goes tense. If he is on a pony this tells the pony to go faster. Squeezing the legs tight and leaning forward tell the pony to gallop. No matter that the rider may be pulling the reins; the pony can ignore that or even use it to brace himself against. It's usually called running away, but as you can see the pony is actually doing exactly what she's asked.

How you move.   This is an extreme case, for the rider is using aids without realising it. But ponies also pick up on much smaller signals. They are particularly sensitive about the way we move: your pony can recognise the way you walk from a long way off. He can also tell what kind of mood you're in, and, as we might expect, is quick to pick up on the slightest sign of nervousness, for that means danger.

I saw this most clearly when I was teaching people to ride. At lunch-time the horses stood in the yard outside the house, able to see people coming down the drive for the afternoon ride. Sometimes they would perk up, looking at the riders with interest; sometimes they looked bored; sometimes they were positively grumpy, hiding behind each other and clearly dreading the ride.

It was only after watching them that I, too, began to see what they were looking at. From the way the riders walked you could see whether they were nervous, bossy, or were the sort of people that horses like, relaxed, gentle and observant. Ponies hate nervousness: to them it means tigers, which means going away, fast. They try to put as much distance as possible between themselves and fear. It never occurs to them (why should it?) that they are the cause of fear; all they can see is that you are advising them to leave.

My horses also disliked the bossy kind of people who think that horses are there to be ordered about. It's fair to say that they weren't like most riding-school ponies, most of which have given up trying to have a relationship with their riders in favour of withdrawing into themselves and sullenly doing the job. My horses were either wild or had had a bad time when they first came to me, so they were particularly sensitive, although no longer nervous. We rode on very steep, difficult mountainsides where horse and rider had to trust each other. It was clear that they felt safe only in the hands of people who would listen to them as well as telling them what to do. The horses, for example, knew much more about bogs than their riders did, and would get sulky if they were kicked hard by riders who thought they were being obstinate when in fact it was not safe to go on.

To my surprise I found that the horses didn't necessarily dislike beginners and like experienced riders. It was not what the riders knew that mattered half as much as what kind of people they were. In their judgement on this they sometimes puzzled me, but almost invariably they turned out to be right. Sometimes, for instance, I thought people were scared when actually they were shy; these people the horses liked far better than I thought they would. Other people would seem to me to be perfectly nice, but the horses hated them. One young German couple who stayed for a week had a poor time riding since the horses refused to do anything with their

Your pony can read your body language too. When you are relaxed and cheerful he will be happy to be with you (right)

If you are loud and wave your arms around a lot your pony will get alarmed by these obvious signs of danger. If he can't go away, or if he knows you better, he will probably decide to ignore you altogether since to his eyes you are simply a fool whose signals are not to be trusted (opposite left)

When you are tense and grumpy your pony will not want to know you (opposite right)

usual cheerfulness. I was disappointed since I liked the couple. But when the time came for them to leave the woman burst out with a passionate and totally weird version of the week's stay: how she knew we were laughing at her behind her back, giving her food she disliked and so on, all of which was untrue and very upsetting. When we tried to reassure her, her husband lost his temper and said we were deliberately trying to drive her mad. When they'd gone (refusing to pay) I went out and congratulated my wise horses.

How horses know these things is difficult for us to understand, since most of us don't read human body language as well as they do. But if you watch them in different people's hands and watch the people they like and dislike, various things become clear.

Fear.   First, of course, is their dislike of fear. This means that you have to conquer any fear in yourself. Unfortunately you can't fool them; they're far too sharp for that. You have to learn to relax. Since tension makes things go wrong between people and ponies (and dogs), it's a particularly important thing to do. Pete will simply not allow himself to be caught or handled by nervous or tense people; he drives them away. It looks like a miracle when another

person strolls straight up to him. When a nervous small boy once tried to give him a carrot, Pete backed away snorting and sweating. His mother, who knew nothing about horses, saw the problem straight away. 'It's the way you're holding it,' she said. 'He can see it's a bomb.' Most ponies are like him, though not all show it so strongly.

It doesn't matter whether you are frightened of the pony himself or tense about other things, for the outcome is still that the pony dislikes the feeling coming from you. You may have noticed that whenever you are in a bad temper ponies always seem to misbehave and make you even crosser. One of the greatest things you can learn from ponies is that they are like a mirror of yourself. Tense, irritable, miserable people make horses tense, irritable and miserable. Happy, open, calm people have joyful horses. So your pony can teach you to become an altogether nicer person.

Relaxing.   You can deliberately practise making yourself relax. First, tense yourself up completely by imagining some desperate situation: crouching in freezing snow watching a pack of wolves plotting to kill you, for instance. Make every muscle as tight as you can. Then let each bit go, starting from your fingers and working up your arms, as if you were letting in a flood of calmness. As you do this you will feel yourself open up: your shoulders drop, your hands open, that crouch disappears and you stand tall and free, like a cormorant drying himself in the sun. Make your breathing deeper and slower, so you are using all of your lungs.

If you practise this just as an exercise you will find that at moments when you are frightened and tense you can catch hold of this feeling. For instance, when you are in a flap because you're late and that pig of a pony has chosen this morning to be uncatchable, find that feeling of complete calm and let it grow in you. Breathe deeply and slowly. Open your shoulders. There's always time, and it saves hours in the long run, for the pony will come to you more trustingly. It's also the best thing to do when you're riding and either you or the pony is nervous, for it stops you from crouching, makes you use your seat better, and tells the pony there's nothing to worry about.

Dealing with fear.   Are you frightened of the pony? The vast majority of people are, particularly at first, so there is nothing to be ashamed of. If you are, try to spend as much time as possible sitting watching ponies. Don't force yourself to fool with them, but take one out to a lush patch of grass and sit reading while he eats, or draw him. The more time you spend with ponies, not fiddling with them but just being with them, the more you will realise what gentle, comfort-loving creatures they are. Don't be afraid of them just because they are large. Unlike you or a dog, they are not by nature attackers, and are unlikely to want to hurt you.

Whenever you have to face fear and overcome it there are two golden rules: first, to find that calmness in yourself before tackling anything, and second, not to ask too much of yourself. If you just force yourself into whatever is scaring you, the chances are that you'll do it wrong and end up even more scared. Instead, try to approach the problem little by little. Work out exactly what it is that scares you, break it down into small steps, and work at each one until you are happy about it before moving on to the next one. (This is the way to teach ponies, too.)

Suppose you are frightened of picking up a pony's back foot because he kicks if you try. Certainly your fear will make him kick all the more. So start by standing close beside him, about level with the back of the saddle, leaning against him with your arm laid along his rump. Relax and think of that good feeling of lying on a beach in the sun. That's all you have to do for the first day. Congratulate yourself, you're making progress. Repeat this for several days, until you both know it's a good safe feeling. Next, relax there before starting to run your hand down towards his hock. Work at that until you're both comfortable about it. Always go back to your 'safe' position between each try and before you leave, and always start there the next day.

Every day, get a little further down his leg. Sooner or later he will lift his back leg; he may even kick. If he does, don't leap away: stay still. If you are standing in the right position, leaning against him, he cannot hurt you, and all you have to do is go slowly back to 'safe' again. When you are both ready, begin again. When he sees that you are not going to be driven away, he will give up kicking. The first time he raises his leg quietly, don't bother about getting hold of his hoof but stop and immediately make a great fuss of him. Give him a reward and lead him away so he sees that making a scene is simply a waste of time.

Every problem involving fear, either yours or the pony's, can be tackled in this way with a bit of thought and planning. You can train yourself out of fear, but you should plan your own training as carefully as you would your pony's. Remember to congratulate yourself every time you master a step, just as you praise the pony. It does not matter whether anyone else finds what you are doing easy; the pony is looking at you, not at them.

Accidents.   The time when it is most natural to be afraid and tense is when there is an accident. They do happen. Ponies get caught in fences, tangled in bridles and blunder into bloody messes in all sorts of ways. With careful thought we avoid most accidents, but wildly improbable coincidences do still arise.

The natural thing to do in an accident is to rush in frantically, trying to calm down the pony without working out what to do. A better way is to stand calmly, not seeing the damage but rather the way out before making a move. A motorcycling friend who went on an advanced driving course said to me: 'The most important thing they taught me was to see the way out rather than the danger.' At that time I used to drive up our narrow lane past a farm where the dogs lay in wait, hearing my bike from far off and plotting violent and often successful attacks on me as I tried to dodge them. The whole road seemed full of teeth and fur. But after listening to Steffan I could see that there was much more road than dog, and that if I watched the spaces instead of the teeth I could sail through them easily. After that I came to enjoy outwitting them.

Horse accidents are like that, too. We have to see the way out, rather than the dreadful things that have happened and the worse ones that might come. A totally wild mountain pony we were trying to round up jumped into a sheep fence and slotted her little legs through the barbed wire and mesh in a horrific way. When we retreated she stopped struggling, knowing it was useless. Five minutes later, after I'd lain down and worked out exactly how to move each leg to free it, I crawled very slowly up the field, very slowly picked up each leg in turn and released her easily – whereupon she took one look at me, went, 'You're a person and I'm terrified of people,' and galloped off without any gratitude. If I'd followed my instinct and run up to her straight away, in a panic, she could have caused herself so much damage that she'd have had to be destroyed, but by giving myself time to see the way out I could go to her without fear. Just as they see fear, ponies can see when we've got the answer, and if we go to them with that written all over us they will calm down enough for us to help them.

Moving calmly.   Other feelings that ponies read clearly from our body language are being in a flap or all hot and bothered. In my experience they don't mind plain misery nearly as much as that flustered frame of mind we can all get into. If you are by nature a flappy, jerky sort of person you will just have to spend hours learning to move as if you were in treacle, or you will find that ponies are never really happy around you. Watch other people

When you rush up to the pony in a panic you will make him panic too, and if he is in difficulties this will make matters worse

If you go up to him looking relaxed, saying 'Oh silly you, never mind, I'll help you out' the pony will probably look sorry for himself and calmly show you what is wrong

carefully, seeing the calm, slow way that good horsepeople move, and try to put yourself in that frame of mind.

There are many stories about difficult, wild-tempered horses being gentle with small children. Maestoso, my Lipizzaner stallion, was so crazy he couldn't be controlled by three grown people, but he had a tiny friend who used to crawl into his stable under the door and pull herself upright using his front legs. She learned to walk by standing between his legs and pulling them forward step by step. Tiny children have no fears, worries or tension, and horses feel good around them. When you go to your pony, leave your worries at the gate and you will find you have no further need of them.

Other moods.   Ponies are also quick to notice when we are dithery or uncertain. All their lives they are taught that we are the ones who decide what to do, and when we can't make up our minds they make up theirs instead. If you pull a pony this way and that, changing your mind about what to do or how to do it, the pony will soon lose patience and do whatever he wants instead.

Many horses, especially sensitive and timid ones, do not like bossy people, the sort that are so busy trying to be master that they don't listen to the horses. Ponies know when we are attending to them; they know when they are being ignored or misunderstood; they feel when they are ridden by somebody who is not thinking about what they are doing. They don't give their best when they are bossed into being obedient. It is sometimes difficult for a beginner to work out how to make a pony do something without being bossy; you need to show him that you have listened to him, that you don't think his objections mean much, and that you still want to do whatever it is. If you say all this out loud, believing it, your body will say it too.

Playing with body language

A fun way to work out what your body language tells your pony is to play with her in a small space. A pen the size of a schooling ring, or half the size of a normal school, is ideal. Let the pony loose. If she is not lively, make a rattle from tin cans or a plastic bag to get her moving. Don't use it when she's coming towards you, only when she's going round or away from you, then she will understand that she can stop the game by walking up to you and standing quietly. You will find that by changing your position, or even the way you stand, you can move her around, excite her, calm

This mare is frantic because her foal has been taken from her to be judged at a show. But her handler remains calm and unflustered. He knows that she is in no mood to listen so he does not try to soothe her or force her to stand still. He stand quietly, as if rooted to the spot. His whole body shows clearly that no matter how much she fusses he will be as immovable as an oak tree

her down or bring her to you. A master of body-blocks and chases, she is aware of exactly where you are. You can shoo her along by waving a hand idly behind her, block her by reaching a hand towards where she is going, and turn her by doing both at the same time. Try waving your hand above your head, crouching down, or ignoring her; try jumping, crawling or taking giant steps.

Many ponies are a bit puzzled by this sort of game at first, but you will find that as you play it more you will get to the point where you are almost dancing together. This is a wonderful way of working with a pony that is excitable when she first goes out, or one that you find a bit much for you, for there is no fear or fight in it. It's more fun than lungeing, and it makes you understand each other more. You have plenty of time to look at your pony's body language and work out what it means; you also have the chance, far more than when you are riding or leading her, to work out what your body language means to her. Once your games are good, put your friends in there instead of you, and watch the pony's reaction.

How sensitive are ponies?

If you don't quite believe that ponies are all that good at telling what we're thinking from the way we move, here's a true story.

Clever Hans was a famous horse that lived in Germany some sixty years ago. He could count and do sums that were shown to him on a card, by pawing the right number of times with his front foot. Of course, everybody thought that his trainer, van Osten, was making a secret sign to Hans to tell him when to stop pawing. But Hans could do the sums even when van Osten wasn't there, in the circus ring for instance. Van Osten himself really believed that Hans could count, and invited scientists to test him.

For a long time Hans baffled them. But then the scientists found that he went wrong unless he was with somebody who knew the right answers. When he was alone, or with somebody who couldn't see the cards, he got the answers wrong.

What Hans was doing was watching the tiny little signs of excitement that people gave when he reached the right number. If you imagine yourself watching him, you'll find that you'd be extra interested in seeing whether he went on pawing after that. Amazingly Hans had worked out, all by himself since van Osten didn't know what he was doing, that by watching these little signs he could get the answers right and get his reward.

Are you as clever as Hans? Ask a friend to think of a number. Count slowly, and see if you can tell when you've reached the right answer. I'll bet you're not as clever as Hans.

Your pony may not be quite as clever as Hans either, but he can certainly tell your mood just by looking at you.

Chapter 7

What's he like?

Pete and Max are as different as chalk and cheese. It's not just the difference in their ages (Pete's twenty, Max six, at the moment), it's their characters. Pete's always been exceptionally sensitive, hating to hurt himself or to put a foot wrong. He's moody, sometimes full of bounce, sometimes dreamy, sometimes grumpy. Max isn't moody: he's always cheerful, bold and energetic. When they go up the mountain together Pete hesitates and calculates, working everything out before he pads over the crags like a cat. Max throws himself at things apparently without looking so that you can't see how he gets his footing right, though he always does. Pete is never headstrong or bargy; you can fence him in with twigs and string that Max would not even think was a fence. Max doesn't mind crashing through things if it means he can frolic off having fun. Of course, Max is a stallion, Pete a gelding, but they would be different anyway.

How much is this to do with the way they're brought up and handled, and how much because they were born with different characters? They were both unhandled youngsters when I got them, and I feel that rather than forcing them to be anything I've let them develop in their own ways. But I also owned Max's father Maestoso for the last ten years of his life, and the differences between him and Max show what handling does.

Maestoso was a highly trained dressage horse; Max isn't. Maestoso had, so to speak, gone to university and done another degree afterwards, where Max is still trying to get his GCSEs. But Maestoso, then thirteen, was an angry, desperate horse. I don't think he'd been outside for years: at first he was surprised by rain and birds. His German trainers had done nothing but train him endlessly, until he'd had enough. He never bit or kicked, but he was determined not to have anything more to do with people than let them feed him. You couldn't catch him in a box, nor put on a bridle and saddle; you couldn't lead him or get on him without several trained helpers: he simply knocked you down with his shoulder and left. He was a sort of mad explosion. It took years of patience and freedom before he lost his need to fight. But people who knew him only later marvelled at his gentle, kingly nature and beautiful manners, as they do at Max's now.

Max, though, has the same streak in him. He cannot bear to be cooped up or punished; once or twice we have had real arguments (mostly about mares) and he does exactly the same things as Maestoso, either leaping in the air or barging you with his shoulder. A few months after I'd first ridden him he went through an awful period of teenage rebellion. He loved to go out; he liked me; being ridden didn't scare him; but he just couldn't see that it should be me that made all the decisions. When we disagreed about where to go next he threw tantrums, leaping, stamping and wriggling. I used to ignore him until he calmed down, then ask him to go on. In the end he realised he wasn't going to get his own way so he might as well give in gracefully. But if I had punished him, as Maestoso had been punished, I would have ended up with the same furious, resentful horse. Max is so like Maestoso (whom he never knew) in his character and ways of doing things that they might almost be the same horse.

What makes up 'character'?

When you meet a pony, then, you are meeting not just his character but all his training and handling too. They are both a part of what he's like. Another part is what is happening to him at the moment. If he is stabled and overfed he will seem quite different to the way he is when he is out at grass.

Sitting at this typewriter, what I am turning out is the character of this book. My publisher, though, can present it to you in different ways. He can choose different types of print, tiny, huge or fancy; give it hard or soft covers; use different paper; print the photos in different ways. He is like the trainer in that what he does makes quite a difference to whether or not you like reading the book. Some books, like some horses, are so badly presented that it's almost impossible to get on with them. Then what you think of the book is also affected by whatever else is going on at the time. If you are sitting in a dark room with the television going full blast

Max is always bold, cheerful and free-moving

reading a book with tiny print, you're not as likely to like it as you would be if you had peace, clear print and a good light.

Every character, pony or person, has ways of living that suit and ways that don't. They all come up happy and smiling if they have been taught the right things in the right way and they are being kept in ways that suit them. They are all capable of pretty awful behaviour if they are treated wrongly. But what suits one pony doesn't necessarily suit another. If we can work out what 'character' is really about, what are the things that a pony inherits from his parents, we have more chance of working out how to handle and train that well.

Inheritance. The sorts of things that seem to be inherited are whether a pony is bold or timid, whether he is sensitive or insensitive, and whether he is calm or excitable. Pete, for instance, is timid, highly sensitive and rather excitable; Max is bold (though not as brave as he thinks he is), not so sensitive, and fairly calm: his excitements are generally because he is a stallion. Most English Thoroughbreds are bold, sensitive and excitable; Arabs are generally timid, sensitive and excitable; most native pony breeds are bold, insensitive and calm, like cobs, though the Welsh breeds are usually more excitable. But of course, there are exceptions within breeds. We can make a pony more excitable by handling him harshly and cruelly, or by feeding him oats; we can encourage a timid pony by teaching him to trust us; but left alone he will show his true character better.

Character types

Imagine, then, a three-year-old come for his first training. He has been brought up with his mother and other mares and foals. At six months he has been halter-broken and weaned; then he has been turned out with other youngsters, handled occasionally and treated well. When he arrives we turn him out in a field, by himself for the first time in his life. What does he do? It depends on his character.

The bold youngster rushes off to explore and find the others he thinks must be there; the timid one takes one look at the unknown and turns back to us, whimpering 'Don't leave me.' The bold and excitable one rushes round more and more, working himself up until he tries to leap the fence or gate, and possibly hurts himself a little. If he is sensitive he gives up trying to escape but goes on galloping until he's tired. If he's less sensitive he crashes through anyway, leaving a trail of blood. The calm horse trots round, calling, until he gives up and starts to eat.

In the days that follow, too, we find that their reactions to this horrible situation (for it is horrible, being abandoned in a strange place for the first time) are different, too. The timid and sensitive youngster turns into the trembling wreck we generally call a nervous pony; the timid, insensitive one gets depressed and mopey. The one that comes out best is the calm, bold one, but he's also the most likely to work out an escape plan. If he's insensitive he'll probably try to barge through us when we open the gate; if he's more sensitive he'll wait for a moment when he can't hurt himself.

Anybody with any sense and kindness would not do this to a youngster, so we'll start again. We've put him in a good paddock next to the group he will join, so he can get to know them without getting hurt. He settles well, and we start our training. Immediately the differences in character stand out. Calm ponies learn much faster than excitable ones; bold ones need firm handling at times; excitable ones are liable to hurt themselves; sensitive ones get terribly upset if they are hurt; timid ones need masses of reassurance and cuddles. All of them, if handled correctly, will be what we want: a friendly horse that does what's asked cheerfully and politely. But

This bright and lively colt is in a field with two others that are not so bold. They team up together but instead of moping by himself he invents games like carrying sticks around and tossing them about

what is right is different for each type of character. A young cob thrives on being thrown into new situations at a rate that would send an Arab potty; an Arab needs slow, patient treatment that would send a cob to sleep.

Getting on with different character types.   Many trainers, and indeed many riders, find that they get on with a certain type or breed of pony better than others. What this usually means is that the way they treat ponies suits a certain type of character better than others. This can be very confusing when you have a problem and go to ask for advice. One person may say you should do this, while another says exactly the opposite. In their own ways they are possibly both right, but they are imagining different kinds of characters. In a horse magazine, for instance, an 'expert' answering letters about difficult behaviour seemed to think most of them could be cured by 'a good hard slap'. This writer was obviously used to bold, calm, insensitive ponies of the cob type, which don't much mind if you hit them; indeed, it may make them pay attention to what you are trying to say. But this advice would be disastrous to anyone with an Arab, which would become a nervous wreck, or a Thoroughbred which, being sensitive enough to be upset by a slap and bold enough to resent it, would soon start attacking you. It was foolish as well as unpleasant advice; perish the thought of that writer coming near Pete, who would have a fit if anyone hit him.

Different types of handling   suit different characters. Try to work out what your pony is basically like. Test him in a completely new situation, like stepping through and over strange things on the ground. Whatever he's like, he'll stop and look. If he then wants to go forward and investigate, he's probably bold. If he wants to back or run away, he's timid. If he likes being the leader of a bunch, he's bold; if he's a follower, he's more timid. From your handling and riding you'll know whether or not he's sensitive, and whether he's excitable or calm. Some ponies have been ruined by bad riding, and others beautifully trained; how sensitive he is to being groomed is a good guide.

A bold pony responds well to being handled firmly, given challenges and pushed into them. A timid pony needs coaxing and showing things are safe: he needs to trust you. If you force him you'll make him worse, not better. A sensitive pony is much trickier to ride than an insensitive one (much nicer, too, once you ride well). If you pull at a rein or push with a leg by mistake while leaning forward to open a gate he'll get flustered; an insensitive

When he comes back to the others, one, the leader of the two, is inquisitive but the other hangs back. When you watch ponies playing you can tell a good deal about their characters. If someone treated this colt harshly he would probably start fighting back; the one with white socks would probably go dull, while the third would get nervous. This colt would like an adventurous life, but the timid one would suit a quiet and gentle person

pony is more likely to ignore your mistakes, just as he's more likely to ignore your bouncing around at a canter if you can't sit down well. An excitable pony 'hots up' at almost anything; you must stay calm whatever happens. Patience is important: when she refuses to do something and starts dancing about, learn to stop, stand her still and calm her down before asking again. In particular, be careful about galloping, for that's wildly exciting. A fresh, excitable pony can be difficult; she's best settled by a long steady trot before you start slower, faster or more demanding work. A calm pony, on the other hand, may need a gallop to wake him up, and gets jollier the livelier you are.

Changing your handling to suit the pony is part of being a good horseperson. Many children who've grown out of their first ponies have a difficult time at first with their second, who doesn't suit the same handling as the first. If the pony doesn't like what you're doing, change the way you're doing it before blaming the pony.

I was once sent a 'problem' Welsh cob, a big, strong, handsome fellow, by a trekking centre who'd bred him and used him for many years. He ran away uncontrollably almost every day. They'd tried working out what he was frightened of, tried changing the bit, and tried to calm him down without any success. However, he didn't seem timid, over-sensitive or over-excitable to me; he seemed a bold, calm sort. In fact it was his boldness that was the problem: he simply liked a good gallop every day, and if we didn't give it him he took it willy-nilly. My helpers liked 'slow ride' days, for one of them would be sent to gallop Soda for two miles before we put beginners on him, when he plodded along meekly. It would have been disastrous to treat Mangas, who was excitable, like that, for he would have gone on galloping unstoppably all day. Soda was clearly not the horse for slow trekking; he went to Buckinghamshire and became a greatly admired hunter.

Experience

But what of your typical middle-aged mongrel pony, who doesn't seem to fit into this neat scheme of character types? What you know of her is that she's wonderful, infuriating, baffling, obstinate and lovable by turns. Sometimes she runs up to you, sometimes she won't be caught; sometimes she's cheerful, sometimes grumpy; there are things she will do, things she won't, and things that depend on her fancy. 'She's a real character,' you say, meaning she does funny little tricks like drinking out of cans or blowing bubbles in her water, or not-so-funny ones like bucking after every jump or diving under low branches.

By the time they are middle-aged, most ponies have had several owners. Often as the pony has got older each owner has had less experience than the last. The trainer has handed him on to a child who can already ride, who sells him to a beginner whose mother used to ride; next comes the totally novice family. He's started with a firm, clear set of rules; praise, reward and understanding have made him eager to do what he's told. But each time he's changed hands the rules have changed. Since he's supposed to know what he's doing, there's no praise when he does it, only anger when he doesn't. There's less reward, more demand, and less certainty in the way he's handled. He's also probably learned a few things that would have been better left unlearned. That old survival instinct starts working in his furry head and he learns to take advantage of beginners. This is not something that younger ponies do, for it's not a natural way of thinking for them. Younger ponies get confused and frightened; they are playful in ways that sometimes don't suit us; they get nervous when they are handled by flustered people; but they're not calculating in the way that older ponies are. The calculating comes only after years of not-too-good handling.

If you watch a group of children at a gymkhana, say, or a rally or even a riding school, you will see what makes ponies sour. All too often the ponies are yanked at, kicked, raced up and down, and generally have enormous demands made on them without any praise or consideration. Small wonder they learn the value of turning their bottoms on you in the field, of the low-hanging branch and the well-timed buck. Most people who have spent time around horses get used to seeing them treated like that, but people who haven't are often astonished at the roughness they're expected to put up with. 'If I was one of them I'd have killed the little brats long ago,' a non-riding friend of mine said, watching a rally. All I could say was: 'They're awfully nice creatures, and the ones that do object end up as dogmeat.'

To keep ponies sweet and willing, whatever their character type, you need to give as well as take. You need to praise and encourage, to show the pony you're happy when she does what you ask, not just go on and on demanding. Ponies don't have the same brain-power as we do but they do have the same sorts of feelings and they, like us, get fed up if they just get yelled at when they make mistakes but never praised when they do well. Many riding-school ponies are totally fed up with being ridden, since for them it is usually uncomfortable and no pleasure at all. They shut themselves up like daisies at night. But when you take them away and warm them with a bit of appreciation and gentleness they come out again, though it takes time.

Wise old ponies.   Many older ponies get fixed ideas about how they should be treated and what life is about, and as they realise the power of a kick or a bite they start using these weapons to train the children round them. One of the best riding masters I have known was a small black Thelwell-type mountain pony called Muffin. In his long life Muffin had first had a kind and gentle owner; after her he'd had a fair amount of abuse, and he wasn't going to put up with any more from children half his age. If over-excited

Muffin, aged about 34, in the mountains where he was born. He was wise and clever, and knew how to look after himself

kids screamed and argued round him he charged at them, a horrible demon of flying black hair and grinning white teeth. If you ran behind him he'd lash out; if you were rough in riding him he'd buck you off or lie down and roll you off, then chase you away; if you carried a stick he'd tear it from your hand and stamp it to bits. At gymkhanas he'd run (and win, often) maybe three races, then sit down on the starting line when he'd had enough. He had jumped willingly and well, but one unfeeling owner had forced him to jump after a bout of laminitis, when his feet hurt, so he dealt with the problem in his usual inventive way: instead of refusing he'd charge up to the jump, stop dead and then, if his poor rider had survived and was trying to crawl back down his neck, leap the jump with miles to spare, land flat on all four feet and put his head down to graze. Not many children wanted to try twice. He knew about being beaten, so he did what was asked; but he often did it in such a way that you'd never ask again.

At first I thought Muffin a horrible and dangerous little brute, but after a while I realised what he was doing, and how cleverly. For he never did the unforgivable: he never hurt the children. He terrorised them, scolded them and made them treat him properly with fearful threats. But the kicks never landed on them; his teeth never actually met round fleeing flesh; he dropped them neatly on soft ground, not stones, and he was tirelessly kind and generous to those who were kind to him. Nice children thought him the sweetest pony they'd ever known; rude ones thought him vile. The only time I saw him hurt someone was at a gymkhana, when he refused to run a fourth race. A large lady official walked up behind him and slapped him on the bottom with her programme. In a flash his back feet landed in her ample stomach. She doubled up, shouting, 'That pony's dangerous, he shouldn't be here,' to which I, trying not to hoot with laughter, could only reply, 'The children know better than to stand behind a strange pony and hit him on the bottom.' True, but not appreciated. She wouldn't have dreamed of doing it to a big horse, and manners are manners however small you are. But I don't think he would have aimed to hit a child. He knew exactly what he was doing.

Muffin was a bold, calm and sensitive pony: he liked to be handled gently and was brave and clever enough to make sure that he was. Other old ponies of the same type think up similar sorts of tricks. But it's their experience of not being treated properly that makes them do it.

Moods

Breeding, experience and age, then, all go to make up character. On a day-to-day level, you also find that your pony treats you differently according to his mood. Some ponies are moodier than others, but all of them are affected by weather, the amount of food and work they have had, whether they are out with others, and their hormones.

Most ponies are friskiest in bright, cool weather: those breezy, shiny days in spring, when the sun comes out after a cold shower, make Pete shy and skip about like a yearling. Heat tends to deaden ponies; they don't mind cold so much, as long as it is dry. But cold rain, when a pony has been standing in it all day, will make him miserable, unwilling to move or even grumpy, while driving rain will make him whip round to protect his face and ears.

Like us, most ponies tend to get grumpy when they are hungry, and cold, hungry ponies are worse. When they are tired they are dull and insensitive. On the other hand, too much food and not enough exercise makes them energetic and excitable. Some foods, like oats and beans, are 'heating' or exciting. It is easy to overfeed and under-exercise a stabled pony, and it often leads to bad behaviour, which may in turn mean that the rider gets scared and exercises him even less. Cutting down on concentrated food calms a pony down; if your pony is excitable, try giving him only hay and a little sugar beet for a few days and see if he changes. Ponies of the same size do not necessarily need the same amount of food: there are 'good doers' and 'bad doers', so it is wise to use the feeding advice given on feed sacks and in books only as an idea to start with. How your pony looks and behaves are better guides to whether he is being fed the right amount.

Some ponies are calmer when they are ridden alone, and some are calmer when they are out with others. Some do not like to go in front, and others hate to be behind. Some jog along happily side by side; some think they are starting a race; some hate other ponies behind them. You just have to find out what suits you and your pony best.

Hormones.   Hormones are chemicals that are produced in certain glands and are carried round the body in the blood. There are many different hormones but the ones that change behaviour most are the so-called sex hormones. Testosterone, the male sex hormone, is produced in the testes so only stallions have it. It makes a horse more energetic and forceful. It also makes him think about mares, and do various things that only stallions do: herd mares, defend them from other males, dung on other horses' dung and so on.

Gelding a colt stops him producing testosterone so he no longer behaves like a stallion, though if he is gelded late, as a three-year-old or later, he may have learned to behave like a stallion and go on doing some of the things stallions do. In rigs, one testis stays in the body and goes on making testosterone, while the other drops in the normal way and is taken off in gelding. The rig, then, looks like a gelding but behaves like a stallion. In fact many of them behave a lot worse than stallions. If you have bought a gelding that attacks other geldings when there are mares about, and generally behaves like a stallion, have a vet test for testosterone in his blood;

Pete in a grumpy mood. It is hot and he doesn't want to be ridden in his own field, so although Jo is being kind and doing nothing wrong he pulls a face and lashes his tail when asked to move. If there were something wrong he would show us, so we ignore his grumpiness and he always cheers up once he's out of his field

if he is a rig, take him back to the seller, for you will never be able to tell when he will behave dangerously.

More testosterone is made in the spring and summer than in autumn and winter. Many stallions are almost like geldings in the winter, getting more stallionish in the spring. We had a Welsh mountain stallion which was ridden by children all winter, with Max and Pete and even mares, but in spring he got so obsessed by thoughts of herding mares and fighting other males that he was no longer safe. Max the stallion and Pete the gelding are great friends and live together in a field or barn all autumn and winter, but in spring Max's games get too rough for poor Pete so they have to be parted. You can actually see the changes that testosterone makes, for stallions grow great crests to their necks and their muscles bulge when they are at their most stallionish.

Mares have female sex hormones that make them come in season during spring and summer, for about five days every three weeks. An egg is made on the next-to-last day, so that is when mating most often leads to a foal. Being in season changes some mares' behaviour a lot, though others don't change at all (see p.75).

Changing

There is not a lot you can do to change the character a pony is born with, though you can change what comes out when you ride or handle him. After twenty years of encouragement Pete is still a timid pony. When I say the ground ahead is safe he goes forward even though he wouldn't if he were on his own, but he does so ultra-carefully. This means I can take him into places that I wouldn't dream of taking a bolder pony, for I can trust him not to hurt himself. If you were to see the mountains he's climbed, the rivers he's swum and the obstacles he's been through you'd think he was a bold pony, but he's not. He isn't nervous, but he's timid.

You can, and do, change a pony's experience, giving her a fresh view of life. When you get a new pony it is months before you really settle down together, for you both need to learn each other's ways. It also takes months or even a year to change the way that a pony thinks about people or work. No ponies are born bad-tempered; they are made that way by bad handling. You can make them better tempered by adding good experiences to the bad, but it will take time before there are more good ones than bad, and during that time the pony will go on being beastly. One grain of sugar doesn't sweeten a cupful of vinegar; you need to go on pouring it in.

In the short term, though, you can often change some sorts of behaviour simply by changing the way that the pony is kept. If she is over-excitable, too energetic or frantic, always change towards a more natural way: give the pony more space, more company, less concentrated food. You can often see the difference in as little as a few days. If the pony seems depressed, she may need more food, company or warmth if bad weather is getting her down.

Chapter 8

Bullies, leaders and friends

If you keep your pony with a group of others in the field, you will notice that there's one horse that's boss over the rest. She drives them away from the food, gets the best place in the shelter, is first at the gate for titbits and is often seen charging at the others with bared teeth, or kicking them away furiously. In a mixed-sex group the boss is usually a mare, and the other ponies fear her.

If we watch a breeding herd of wild ponies or mustangs, living in wide-open spaces where there are no piles of food to be fought over, no haynets or buckets, no gates, fences or titbits, we see something that seems to be the same. There's hardly any kicking or biting, much less than in tame ponies, but there is one mare that is the leader. When they go from place to place it is she who starts moving first, while the others fall into line behind her with the stallion at the back rounding up the stragglers like a sheepdog. When there is an alarm it is she whom they all watch, and often she who gives the sign that they should move or relax.

With our ideas that bosses are the ones that give orders and the rest are the ones that fall into line behind them, we naturally assume that the boss mare in a tame herd would be the leader mare if the herd were wild. But we are wrong. The boss mare is the one that the others fear and have learned to give in to; the leader mare is the one that they trust and follow. They run away from the boss, but they follow the leader. Boss and leader are not the same horse.

One group

I kept one group of horses and ponies together for several years. Sometimes they were kept in fields, ridden and fed; other times

they were turned out on the mountain for months so they were
more like a wild herd. They were: middle-aged Tess, a heavy, hairy
Irish vanner who did all our farm work; young Emma, a big,
timid half-Arab; young Sophie, an Irish hunter who came from the
gypsies looking like a toast-rack; old Mangas, the crazy black and
white cob; young Pete, and Dink the donkey. It was natural that
the young mares, both of whom had had a hard time, should trust
and follow Tess, who was a comfortable soul. It was also natural
that they, being timid, should give in to her about food, though
she was not a bossy sort. In turn these two, who appeared to be
totally in love with each other the way that fellow sufferers often
are (they would eat from the same bucket together, then move over
to the next together), were very spiteful towards poor Pete, who

Hungarian csikos rider with eight horses. The rows of horses are tied together,
but nothing connects each row to the one behind, so he is truly controlling them
all. In this type of event the relationships of the horses is important. The front
ones must be naturally bold leaders, the others content to be followers, and
all the horses in one row must be friends

was always a wimp in company, and perfectly horrible to Dink. They left Mangas well alone. Dink then took shelter under Tess's comforting bulk where she was protected, and the two geldings teamed up.

Mangas was a wise old bird and he and Pete, who was inquisitive and bright, were great friends. Mangas never bossed Pete, but Pete, who eats slowly, would always give him the last of his food. They had tremendous races: when we were out riding they'd prance along shoulder to shoulder, eyeing each other until at some tiny signal they'd be off in a mad race that Pete always won. When he drew ahead Mangas would deliberately shoot off to one side so Pete had to wheel and scamper after him, so it was a game of wits as well as speed. But loose on the mountain it was always Mangas who followed Pete as he explored the crags.

Into this group came Little Hawk, who was four. Tiny and unbelievably tough, she was the wildest pony I've ever met, born and raised in a totally untouched mountain herd. We tamed and rode her, though her spirit remained wild and free. From the first day

she mercilessly bossed everybody, though they were all far bigger than her. She bullied Tess and kept Emma and Sophie trembling; Mangas kept as far away as possible, and Pete hid behind him. The only one she didn't boss was Dink, as though it was beneath her. She never had a close friend, though she stayed by Tess while Dink hid round the other side.

Hawk, then, was certainly the boss; but Tess was the leader. No one followed Hawk anywhere: they were glad to get rid of her. Mostly Tess would amble off with Hawk jealously guarding her and Dink trotting the other side; Sophie and Emma would follow, then Mangas and Pete. On the mountain Tess would sometimes stop, puzzled, and Pete would show her the way over the difficult bits. But when there was a sneaky escape it was Dink who started it, Tess who followed, and then the rest. Tess loved Dink; when Dink first arrived all the others were terrified of her (horses who haven't seen donkeys usually are: they seem to think a witch has got at a pony, and the result might be catching) but Tess, perhaps remembering a friend from her Irish home, called to her as a mare calls to her foal.

Out on a ride, the order was different. Mangas and Pete went first, looking for a racetrack; the two young mares came next, Sophie first as she was the bolder; Tess lumbered behind; Dink got under everyone's feet in gateways, and Hawk flew up and down the line chivvying everyone. In the races she went on where Mangas and Pete stopped, for she could skip over ground that even Pete couldn't gallop over; then she'd turn on a sixpence and prance back to snort at the boys. The children who survived riding Hawk all turned out fearless, with exceptionally good seats.

When we went to catch them Emma, Sophie and Pete would run up to me; Tess would stand to be caught, Hawk allowed herself to be bribed and Mangas was totally uncatchable. If he had a chance he would round up all the others and try to block them from coming. Usually one of the others sneaked round him, but if they were in a jolly mood he'd keep them running by herding them like a stallion. For years we never did catch him in the field. Once we'd got the others he'd follow, terrified of being left alone, and come after us meekly to the yard and his bucket.

On camp, we turned these friendships and ties to our advantage. For if we tethered Dink, Tess stayed, so the other two mares did too (as they got older and bolder they would go off, so we tethered Emma). If we tethered Pete, we had Mangas. And Hawk would trot about seeing that everybody was behaving, when she wasn't rummaging in the tents.

What we had were typical examples of the ways that horses feel about each other. They can be friends like Sophie and Emma; they can be leaders, like Tess; or they can be bossy like Hawk. Friends and leaders keep the group together; bossiness drives them apart. In a breeding herd another thing keeps them together: family. Yearlings and two-year-olds, as well as foals, tend to hang around their mothers, though they go off with their friends as they get older.

If you think about children in a group, say at school, you can see the same relationships. Friends, leaders and bullies exist there, too. Your friend is someone you want to be with and do things with, for you like their company. You usually obey the bully, out of fear; but if you have any sense you avoid him unless you think that sucking up to him is a better way of avoiding pain. But in any difficulty the person you trust and follow is not necessarily your friend and it is unlikely to be the bully. Bossiness in people, as in ponies, is not attractive.

How ponies feel about us

Since these kinds of feelings about each other are natural to ponies, it is natural they should feel them about us, too. There are ponies who are real friends with their owners, liking to be near them, to touch and be touched by them. When you let go or fall off them they don't go away: they hang about, for they are happy to be around you. Next door's pony, who lives in the same field as me, moons about my front door, coming in to nuzzle my head while I type; she dozes beside me when I sit outside; and you can lie against her when she lies down, for she feels no threat from people. But friendly ponies like this are often the ones that don't necessarily do what they're asked, just as you don't necessarily fall in with what your friend wants to do. If you are good friends with your pony you may expect little tiffs from time to time, and a bit of teasing and playfulness from her; but you can be sure she will not hurt you and that at times she will protect you. Like a friend, she may feel free to make the decisions when she thinks she knows better than you. But to have a pony that really likes to be with you is a great pleasure.

Then there are ponies that are bullied by their owners. I have seen this more in bigger horses, for some adults treat a horse like a machine or a toy they play with, ignoring his feelings; children seem more naturally to go for the idea of being friends with their ponies, at least until they're told they must 'teach the pony who's master'. It's not difficult to bully a horse once you've discovered how: they don't like being hurt and although their usual way of dealing with bullies is to go away, the next best move if you can't leave is to shut up and do what you're told, whether you're a person or a horse. If you have been in that situation yourself you will know it makes you go dead and dull inside: there's no spark, no interest and no pleasure in working like that. I have seen many horses like this; they do become like machines. The timid and sensitive sorts get nervous, hopelessly anxious to please, like people who suck up to bullies.

There are a few horses who, like Maestoso, simply won't give in to being bullied. Mostly they come to unfortunate ends, for they become dangerous to be around. Handling a horse like that without hurting him further, or getting hurt yourself, is terribly difficult: you have to plan every move with care yet appear totally carefree, so that the horse realises that you are not afraid of him nor need he be of you. These horses think that anything to do with people is a question of who can hurt the other first, or more. It's difficult to convince them that life is far simpler and a lot more fun.

The third way that ponies feel about each other is as leaders and followers. Every group has a leader, generally one of the older mares. Even between a pair of friends there may be a leader and a follower if one is much bolder than the other.

Usually we break in ponies when they are three years old. In a wild horse's life this is the time when he will start to go away from the herd, exploring in the company of friends. They follow the bravest; at times when one loses his nerve they literally put their heads together and get courage from each other, or they run back to the herd and its real leader. If a pony of that age is taken from his group and goes out with a calm, bold, clear person who shows him many new things, he naturally comes to rely on that person as a leader. After all, the person knows a lot more about what is going on than he does. If the pony is then treated decently and sensibly he will go on thinking of people as leaders for the rest of his life.

A good leader

When we are doing something as a group and need a leader, what we look for is someone whose judgement we can trust, who doesn't lose his cool or get into a flap, who doesn't change his mind every ten seconds. We don't expect him to have eyes in the back of his head, but we do expect him to listen when we notice something worrying that he hasn't. When we take our fears and doubts to him he doesn't just tell us to shut up: he considers them. He may change his plan because of what we have seen, or he may explain why we need not worry about it. He is determined: when he makes a plan he carries it through. And it works. That is why we do what he tells us.

This is exactly the type of person that ponies like best. They like good leaders, they like to be able to trust someone and they are then perfectly happy to do what they are told, without being threatened or punished. They particularly need good leaders when they are young, faced with all sorts of things they know nothing about, in an unnatural world where the knowledge in the backs of their minds is no help. Timid ponies go on needing good leaders all their lives, but a bold and clever pony who has learned to cope with our world may, as she gets older, decide that the leadership is better with her than with a weak, foolish or dithery person. If you are a beginner, then, you may find that the pony you bought as being well-behaved is leading you off in all directions; but as you get more sure of yourself she will be willing to follow your leadership.

Family ties

The fourth type of natural bond between horses is that of mother and foal, and again they sometimes treat us like mothers or foals. Orphan foals that have been bottle-fed come to follow people and to think of them as mothers. This is charming in a foal but awful later on. As they grow up, these youngsters start playing with people as they would with their mothers and friends, rubbing on them, jumping on them, nipping them and generally playing far too rough for our liking. The best place for an orphan once he is weaned is out with other ponies, who will teach him manners far better than we can.

Some mares even treat us like foals. My friend's mare on a long journey together shows a lot of motherly behaviour towards him. Not only does she stand guard over him at night; she calls him with that especially low nicker that mares use to call their foals, and when he stands beside her she constantly turns to touch him with her nose as a mother does to her foal. It might be truer to say that I know a mare that owns a friend of mine. He notices particularly that when they are on the mountain, The Steed, who is a hot little mare, is certain that she knows best; but when they hit the road she is like a lamb, as if she knows that this is his world and she must trust him.

When we released Pete into Mangas's field after a long separation, Pete ignored Mangas and instead trotted off to explore, with Mangas trotting behind. At first we thought Pete hadn't recognised his old friend (Photo: Jane Turner)

Confusions

As in the other things they do, the way that ponies treat us fits into their natural way of thinking. We can be bosses, leaders, friends or even family; most often we are a mixture, which can be confusing for both of us sometimes. What is certainly confusing for a pony is to be treated one way one day and another the next. This always happens, of course, when they change hands, and if you treat a pony differently from her last owner she will take weeks or months to get used to this new idea, though she will. A pony that has always been treated in a harsh and bossy way will at first not understand what is happening when you treat her as a friend, and you may be disappointed that she does not seem to appreciate your kindness; but in time she will.

Ponies also find it confusing if, having treated them as friends, you suddenly decide to go in for some rather bossy schooling. It can be done, but the pony understands the change much better if it always happens in a particular place and always starts in the same

Pete wanted to meet Floyd, the cream horse, but Mangas blocked him and drove Floyd away with a warning head-thrust, which scared Floyd (Photo: Jane Turner)

way. Going to a special place and always beginning by trotting in circles, say, are signals to the pony that you want her to behave in a certain way. After she has got the idea, simply trotting in circles anywhere will be a good enough signal. Once he had calmed down, Maestoso even knew that different tack signalled different ideas: when he wore a vulcanite snaffle I didn't mind if he was playful or if he suggested going a certain way, having a gallop or even stopping to eat; but when he wore a double bridle I expected him to be a dressage horse that did only what he was told.

Old friends

People often wonder how much ponies remember old friends. When you meet a pony you've known well years before you may be disappointed to find that he doesn't appear to recognise you. But I think they don't forget. I once had a job in a place overlooking a field where there was a small bay pony. On my way to work the

Pete finally got his way. But Floyd, who was a timid three-year-old, had been so frightened by Mangas's threats that he mouthed at Pete. Mangas was quite ready to attack again if Floyd tried to go off with Pete (Photo: Jane Turner)

pony spotted me, neighed, galloped over and seemed pleased to see me. During the day I could see other people pass and his owner arrive but he did not do the same to them, so I realised there was something special about me. Several days later I remembered him: I'd had him for six months many years earlier when he was a scared, underfed three-year-old. He'd grown, filled out and was happy, but he knew my walk instantly.

I think ponies are particularly pleased to see us again if they remember us as being kind to them after a bad time. But they also remember when they don't appear to. Mangas and Pete were parted for some ten years and we were all agog to watch their pleasure when they met again. But when we delivered Pete to Mangas's field, to our astonishment he completely ignored Mangas, instead running round the field and greeting the horses next door. Eventually he settled down and started eating, while Mangas strolled over and nuzzled his back in their old way. It was some time before the penny dropped. Of course Pete recognised Mangas, just as well as

Once he had met Floyd, Pete lost interest, and instead turned to groom Mangas as he always had years before. Mangas is in his mid-thirties in these photos, and as lively as ever (Photo: Jane Turner)

he did when they lived together. But what excited him were the new things, not old Mangas whom he knew so well. They didn't need to greet each other, any more than they did after they had been parted for only five minutes. Perhaps this is why, when we meet our old ponies years later, they make less fuss over us than over a person they've never met before: they know exactly who we are, and do not need to be introduced.

Titbits

Hunting animals often bring back goodies to their friends and mates. Offers of food, which takes an effort to get, are sure signs of friendship. For grazing animals they aren't because their food is all around them. Ponies, then, don't understand titbits the way you mean them. Their idea of friendship is being close, touching one another and scratching each other's withers and tail. If you want to be friends with a pony, do it the pony's way.

Some gentle ponies stay sweet however many titbits you give them, but others don't: they get greedy and nippy. On the whole, you're better keeping your titbits for times you are using them as a reward for the pony's good behaviour: for coming up to you in the field (always), for being patient with the blacksmith, or for learning something new.

Chapter 9

Learning and teaching

During the thirty or so years of his life a pony never stops learning. It is true that older ponies, like older people, can get rather fixed in their ways, but if they change hands late in life they are just as quick to learn their way around a new place and a new owner's habits as is a young pony. 'You can't teach an old dog new tricks' is not true: they are always able to learn. The question is whether we give them the chance, and how easy we make it for them.

There are different kinds of learning that we expect from a pony. He learns not to be afraid of all sorts of things that naturally scare him; he learns not to hurt us; and he learns what to do when we give certain signals. As well as this he quietly gets on with learning things he thinks are far more important, like where his food is stored, how to find his way around in the dark, how to undo stable doors and so on.

Learning to learn

Although these kinds of learning are rather different, it is true of all of them that the more a pony has learned, the quicker he learns a new thing. Like other animals, and us, ponies learn to learn. One of the reasons why Pete is so clever and quick about solving new problems is that he has faced and worked out thousands of them in his varied lifetime. He knows, for instance, that door handles open doors so it seldom takes him more than five minutes to learn how to open a new one (though I have found him trying to use the knocker instead); he has been trained in so many different ways that he could learn another with ease. At twenty his mind is as alert and teachable as a three-year-old's. Trigger, the famous trick horse of the screen cowboy Roy Rogers, lived to a ripe old age and was still able to learn a new trick within a couple of hours. So if you want your pony to get brighter, start teaching him, whatever his age.

Teaching a pony not to be afraid

The first kind of learning, how to get over natural fears, usually comes early in a pony's life. It is a weird fact that most of the things we want to do with ponies are exactly what naturally scares them most: put snakey ropes round their heads so they can't run away, tie them up, get hold of their feet, shut them up by themselves in dark boxes, cling on to their backs like lions, tie them into carts that chase them from the scary place behind them that they can't see, and so on. In this kind of learning we break down the pony's fear gradually, praising or rewarding him at every stage so that he learns to feel comfortable with things that the back of his mind tells him are scary. Anger and punishment are absolutely out of place, for they only frighten the pony more.

Preparations: breaking down the problem.   Before you start work, think about the problem and how you are going to break it down into steps. You do not want to panic the pony by doing too much at once; by getting him used to things little by little you can help him control his fear. If you get straight on to an unbroken pony, for instance, he is likely to panic and buck you off. Instead, you start off by leaning on him, then over him, then lying over him; you get him used to walking about with you draped over him before you sit on him normally. He gets comfortable with each of these steps before you move on to the next. Every problem can be broken down into steps in this way.

   Secondly, try to make sure that if the pony does leap about in panic he is not going to hurt himself. Wheelbarrows, pitchforks, open doors or anything else he might crash into should be tidied away. If things go right this work will not have been necessary but you never know when something totally unexpected and stupid might happen at exactly the wrong moment.

Be relaxed.   When you know that what you are going to do will worry the pony, you must be calm, relaxed and certain yourself. If you leap back and give up as soon as she starts making a fuss, you will only tell her that she is quite right to be scared. It's also true that if you try to force her you will scare her more. Somewhere

Undoing stable doors is one of the things that ponies teach themselves

between these two extremes is a middle way of quietly doing a little, praising the pony, standing back to let her relax and realise that she hasn't been harmed, and then going on.

The lesson.   Suppose you want to teach a pony to let you handle her feet. Of course, you are not going to expect her to hold up her foot for five minutes, as she will do when being shod, the first time you try to pick it up. You are going to expect a lot less. How far you get in your first lesson will depend on how scared she is.

   To help the pony feel confident, work with her in a place she knows she is safe, and start by doing something she already knows. Grooming and rubbing her always makes a good start to a session, since you are showing the pony your friendship. Quite casually, put your hand on her shoulder and start running it slowly down her leg. She will steadily get more nervous until, as you reach her knee or below, she snatches her foot away. This is the point where you praise and reward her, for actually she has done half of what you wanted: she has picked up her foot. The fact that you wanted her to do it slowly, with your hand round it, doesn't matter at this stage. What does matter is that you praise her for getting even a small bit right, and that you let her stand and think about it. After a minute of comforting chat, you try again. This time she will probably snatch her foot away a little less quickly. After several goes, several rewards and lots of praise she will be lifting her foot quite calmly and may even let you hold it for a second. At this point her lesson is over, and you can start again the next day.

Repeating the lesson.   Fear is a funny emotion. You can wear it down by working away at it, like water dripping on a stone, but unlike stones it has a habit of growing again overnight. The day after a pony has 'learned' to pick up her feet calmly she is quite likely to have 'forgotten' her new trick, and you have to begin all over again. What you find, though, is that the second time she learns quicker than the first, and so on. In order to get rid of her fear entirely you have to keep working, and keep practising for a long time even after it seems to have disappeared entirely. This is not really surprising when you remember that all her lifetime the pony has been carefully practising the exact opposite, for the back of her mind tells her never to get her precious feet caught in anything.

Praise and reward.   Praise is particularly important since it makes the pony relax; being yelled at, even when he seems to be being silly just for the sake of it, only adds to his fear. If you imagine yourself trying to do something that terrifies you, you will realise the same is true for you. Being bullied might make you do it, because you were more frightened of the bully than of the thing itself, but you'd still be scared. A kind person who said how brilliant you were would make you feel good about doing it.

But praise is important to ponies for another reason, too. They don't have the faintest idea what we want. This is not something we usually remember. We know we want to pick up the pony's foot, but for all he knows we might want him to keep it on the ground, paw, shake hands, dance about or any number of strange things. We might even want to cut it off. We humans do have batty ideas from a pony's point of view, and a young pony has no hope of guessing what we might dream up next. Praising a pony when he makes a move, however slight, in the right direction is the only way we have of showing him what we think the right direction is.

Different ponies.   While all ponies are afraid of much the same things, some are more afraid than others. Some ponies really hate water; some are really head-shy. People often think that a particular pony has had a dreadful experience to make him especially afraid. This may be true, but it is also true that ponies simply vary, as people do. Most people don't feel happy standing on the edge of a cliff; quite a large number are very scared, and a small number are absolutely terrified. These people suffer badly from vertigo, some so much that they can't even climb a ladder or stand on a chair. Probably all of us feel vertigo to some extent, but only a few do so badly.

Ponies, too, vary. They are almost all naturally wary about water; rivers, after all, can be dangerous, full of slippy stones, mud, hidden pools and alligators. Ponies need to be taught to overcome this fear. You may buy an older pony whose previous owner has said 'oh, he won't cross water' and left it at that. In cases like this you have a longer job on your hands, for the pony has had a longer lifetime of avoiding water, and has been allowed to think he is right, so his determination will be stronger. Clearly, you will need twice the determination and twice the praise to get him over it, though you will in the end; but he may go on disliking water, even if he doesn't actually fear it, until he dies. (I have, however, met horses that loved water. Fred, a young stallion from the Arizona desert, had never seen water except in a bucket until we arrived at the bank of a big river at midnight, to camp there. Being thirsty, Fred drank eagerly, strolling out into the river until he pulled me off my feet. He spent the next half-hour swimming about merrily

When you and the pony are learning something new that frightens both of you, stay calm and take your time. It may take you a week to work through all the steps you need before you can pick up his back feet.

Stay close to the pony, with your bodies touching and your arm on his rump. This is your 'safe' position. Get both of you to relax here

Run your arm down his rump, quite firmly and not too slowly. If he objects, go back to 'safe' and relax before starting again. Always stay close. If you jump aside you will suddenly appear within his vision and will look frightening

Keep going a little further each time until you reach his heel. If he kicks, take no notice but go back to 'safe' and start again. He *cannot* kick you if you are standing in this position, so don't worry. Don't punish him for kicking, especially if he is young. It is a perfectly natural thing for him to do. When he realises that kicking isn't getting rid of you he will give it up if he senses that you are calm and there is nothing to be feared.

If he will not pick up his foot, put your hand round the back of his fetlock joint and pull it towards you. If you push against his hip with your shoulder you will rock his weight on to the other foot and help him lift this one

Finally, turn his foot back so you can see underneath it. Rubbing his foot and patting the sole, praising him warmly as you do so, will make him understand what you wanted.

Now make a big fuss of him . . . and yourself

in the dark. We let him swim, free, by himself, for hours every day after that. But he was a curious fellow anyway, given to sucking the wing mirrors of cars like giant lollipops.)

Bad experiences.   As well as natural fear, ponies sometimes have to be taught to get over traumatic fear. This is the kind of fear, often panicky, that comes after an accident or terrible incident. It is particularly difficult to get over, and often takes years. As a yearling Pete had an accident when a narrow metal gate, the kind with spikes on top, unexpectedly fell on him, got tangled in his halter rope and kept leaping at him and spiking him. He is still, nineteen years later, so scared of this kind of gate that he usually dashes through them and often bangs himself, proving to himself that he is right and they do hurt.

Black Jack, a charming, gentle cob, had had some awful experiences before I bought him as an unbroken three-year-old to save him from going for meat. He was terrified of a hand going towards his head and would even strike out with his front feet if he was cornered and someone tried to catch him. When we'd managed to get a headcollar on him I used to catch him by letting him feed from a bucket under my arm and clipping in the lead rope while he couldn't see my hand. For months he would follow me, nuzzle me, play with me, love to be ridden, and refuse to let me reach out towards his head. It took two years of kindness before you could go up to him in the normal way, though he'd run up to you quite happily as long as your arms were folded.

Jack never managed to explain what had happened to him. Although he was wild he'd been gelded, heaven only knows how, and I guess that in his fear and pain he'd somehow fixed all the blame on hands going towards his head. He never was afraid of someone going behind him or reaching underneath him, which might seem to make more sense. But traumatic fear often is rather senseless. When I was eight I almost drowned in the sea when someone turned over a rubber dinghy on top of me and I kept coming up underneath it. Luckily a skilled lifesaver was near, or I shouldn't be here now. It would seem sensible for me to be afraid of the sea or boats but I swim and sail fearlessly; what does terrify me is to swim near strangers, for I *know* that they will duck me or pull me under, and no amount of doing it has made me less afraid.

Fortunately not many ponies have had dreadful experiences, but when they have we sometimes find that the normal ways of quietly going on and praising any progress don't work. The pony doesn't get better: he gets so that he doesn't want us anywhere near him, in case we should start doing that dreadful thing again. When this happens, and I would stress that it is rare, the best thing we can do is to avoid the scary thing and instead concentrate on teaching him to get over lots of other fears. With Jack I did lots of work with his feet, with going round his back end, with riding him through and over all sorts of difficult places (in a headcollar, for I couldn't put a bridle on him), until he had learned to trust me. All of a sudden one day he decided even my hands were harmless. Unfortunately I then sold him to a girl I thought more sensible than she really was, and two months later he was back, worse than ever even with me. It was a little girl of eight who got him over it the second time, which just goes to show that you do not have to be old and know a lot; you just need patience, common sense and a lot of kindness. Incidentally, she now owns him.

Learning not to hurt us

A second kind of learning is learning what *not* to do, like bite or kick. Again, most ponies learn this early in life. Actually very few of them, if they have been well handled, ever do bite or kick, and the wilder they are the less likely they are to do it. Usually it is youngsters that have been over-petted, so that they have no respect for people, who do it, for they treat us like their playmates whom they bite and kick for fun or out of irritation. It's no fun for us, for we're a bit more fragile.

If you watch young ponies playing you'll see them run up to an older mare and bite her on the rump for fun. She will immediately lash out or whip round to bite them. This fast and furious punishment teaches them to leave her alone. Since that's what they understand, we should do the same.

Timing your punishment.   What we have to notice especially is that if the mare misses, she doesn't wait until they come around again and then attack them: she just ignores what has happened, though she keeps an eye out in case they should try again, so that she'll be ready next time. What is important here is timing. If your pony nips you it is no use clutching your arm, seeing how badly he's bruised you and then going to hit him. In these brief seconds he will have forgotten all about it and will just be astonished, upset and even angry when you attack him out of the blue. For in order for the pony to make a connection between what he has done and being punished for it, the punishment must arrive *as he is doing it*. If you hit him when he is standing quietly then you are punishing him for standing quietly, not for biting you half a minute before-hand.

We are often punished for things long after we have done them, so we find it difficult to understand why ponies seem to be particularly thick about it. But a moment's thought will show that when you are scolded for something after you have done it you are always told why. If you were scolded without being told why you would be as puzzled and resentful as ponies are, unless you'd already guessed the reason. You can't tell a pony what you are scolding him for and he's unlikely to guess the reason, so if you punish him you must make sure that the reason is completely obvious. The only way you can do that is to punish him when he is in the middle of doing wrong.

Older ponies.   If you have an older pony that bites or kicks it is quite possible that people before you have punished him at the wrong moment, so that he has learned that people are dangerous, unpredictable creatures that ought to be driven away before they hurt him. A pony like this needs to be taught not to be afraid of you, and that means you must not be afraid of him either. I know it's difficult. Often what you have to do is to arrange things so that he really cannot do it, so that you feel comfortable. You will find that with constant kindness his behaviour and the way he thinks about you will change, although it will take months.

Some ponies, like Pete, bite when the girth is done up roughly or they are brushed in ticklish places. This is because they are thin-skinned and do not want to be hurt. They cannot bite if you tie them up, but you should also use a soft or padded girth and do it up slowly and gently. Here the pony is actually punishing you for not treating him properly, so it is your behaviour that has to change, you who have to learn.

Punishment.   Learning what not to do, then, can depend on punishment. It is the only kind of learning that does, and even then you have to be absolutely sure that punishment is really what is needed and that you are doing it at exactly the right time. The most savage horses I have known were ones that had been punished at the wrong moments. At the French National Equestrian Centre at Saumur I was talking to some eminent dressage experts with my back to a horse's box. 'That horse is savage,' they said, but I got too interested in the conversation. Suddenly the horse sank his teeth into my shoulder and didn't let go. I immediately sank my teeth into his tender nose and didn't let go until he did. I could hear him go away snorting and stamping, but two minutes later he did it again. This time I was even quicker and fiercer. He went away to think, came back and stood with his mouth open above my shoulder. I showed him my teeth. 'I thought so,' he nodded, and then, ever so slowly, lowered his nose until he was touching me, with his mouth closed. I relaxed, and for the next twenty minutes he nuzzled gently at me, playing with my hair and licking my neck, while everybody passing by gaped as if I'd had my head in a tiger's mouth. This was a stallion who wanted desperately to touch people but had been a bit rough, got punished at the wrong moments, and had become confused and angry. Luckily my strange punishment had hurt him exactly when he hurt me, and he was then clever enough to work out exactly what was allowed. Poor horse, when they wanted to catch him they'd go in waving a stick until he gave up trying to get them and stood cowering in a corner. All he wanted was a touching game.

Another young stallion I broke in so loved to go out that when you went in the box with his bridle he came at you with his mouth open wanting to have the bit put in. When I saw him again a year later he was an angry, dangerous horse; his innocent eagerness had been wrongly punished by people who thought he was trying to attack, and after he'd been hurt he really did attack, viciously. It took some time to sort out the confusion.

Be careful when you punish a horse, for it can teach him to be savage if you do not get it right. On the whole a pony that has been well treated never needs to be punished. It is appalling to see so many ponies beaten and yelled at when such punishment cannot improve matters. Usually the problem is not that the pony is doing something wrong but that he is not doing what his rider asks. The answer is for the rider to improve his riding, his understanding of why the pony is refusing, and his temper. Being beastly to ponies does not make them understand you better or want to listen to you; it just makes them even more grumpy.

Learning what to do

The third type of learning is learning to do something when asked. Here, reward, praise and patience are what you need; again, anger and punishment confuse and upset the pony, making him tense. Since tension makes a pony fight back against the aids instead of yielding to them, you both need to be as calm and relaxed as possible.

In helping Pony Club children teach their ponies how to side-step (full pass) I have been struck by how few children understand how to teach. They have a go at applying the right aids; nothing happens, since a fifteen-year-old pony faced with this strange demand is likely to think his rider has gone batty. They try moving the pony in the other direction; they get cross and yell at the pony; they try in the first direction again; finally they give up, wailing: 'He won't do it.' In fact I've never met a pony that couldn't be persuaded to side-step quite well with an hour or two's work. I can't imagine those children learning anything if I taught them in the same crazy manner.

Showing what you want.   When a pony does not understand what you are asking him you have to praise and reward him if he even leans in the right direction. This is his only clue as to what you think the right direction is. You then relax completely, letting him do the same, so that the idea can sink in. After a moment you try again, repeating exactly what you were doing before in the same way. He will almost certainly do what brought pleasure to him before. This time you say 'good' and push him a little more before rewarding him; aim to get him to respond a bit more before you praise and relax him. If you carry on in this way you will have the pony moving a step or two in the right direction within a few minutes. You then take him away, have him do something easy that he enjoys or even just wander about for five minutes before bringing him back to the same place and starting again. Keep working at it for a few minutes at a time, asking for a little more before relaxing him, and finishing each little bout with a five-minute relaxation quite away from the problem.

What many children do wrong is to ask too much, praise too little, and forget completely about relaxation; they also get too agitated and change their minds too often so that the pony ends up totally flummoxed, rooted to the spot. You cannot teach a pony anything unless you make it clear what you want. At first you want only a little; if she gets that right you can ask more, but you can't expect her to behave as if she were fully trained the first time you ask. Success does not come all at once: you build it up in steps, just as you broke down the pony's fear in steps.

Making it easy.   Always make it easy for the pony to do the right thing and difficult or even impossible to do the wrong thing. This often means you have to choose your spot and moment carefully, and you may find it easier with a helper. If you are teaching her to side-step, put her sideways across a narrow lane or corridor, so she cannot go forwards or backwards, and have your helper push her sideways as you give her the aids; if you are teaching jumping, make your jumps half a metre high and five metres wide; if you are teaching her to lunge, start in smallish circles, slowly, with your helper leading her on the outside. Do not get angry if the pony does the 'wrong' thing, but calmly start again until she realises there is only one way that will lead to her reward and pleasure.

Putting the pony in a listening mood.   It is also important that you choose your time carefully. It is absolutely no use asking a pony anything, especially something new, if she is in no mood to listen. If there is too much going on around her, or if she is fresh so that all she can think about is playing, or if she is tired, hungry, or just parted from her friend, she is not going to pay much attention to you. Working her quietly for half an hour, running through the things she already knows, puts her in the mood for learning.

Time to relax.   If you think about your own learning you will realise that if you are rushed into new things you don't learn well. You need time to absorb new ideas, time to turn them over and compare them with what you already know. The same is true of ponies. Giving a pony a few moments to relax is a reward in itself, but it also makes her learn better. Asking her to repeat what she has done a few times makes the point clearer. If she then turns to other things for a short while she will not get bored with repeating her new lesson, but will return to it with pleasure.

Repeating.   You will also know from your own learning that you have to repeat it several times over the next few weeks to get it to sink in properly. If you learn something fast, like picking up a new language on holiday, you forget it just as fast unless you keep using it for a while. Once you have got it to set properly you don't forget it completely even if you don't use it for years, though you do get a bit rusty and need reminding at first. Ponies are the same. When they are learning something new it is best if you repeat the lesson the next day, a couple of days later, and after that twice a week for a month or two. For some reason this works better than repeating it every day. Ponies get fed up if they have to repeat the same difficult thing every day (so would you) and they will often start doing the wrong thing even when they know what the right one is. It may just be that learning works best when repeated this way; we know that animals learn better if they have ten lessons spread over ten weeks, a bunch together at the beginning with the others more spread out, than if these ten lessons are squashed into two or ten days. For some reason, having seventy lessons in ten weeks works no better than having ten. So in between your lessons, have a lot of fun with your pony and he will find his learning more fun too.

Place.   Place, as well as timing, is important. Ponies learn best if they are taught in a quiet corner where there's not much else going on to catch their attention. They remember what they have learned much better if your repeat lessons happen in the same place. At first this is a great help, for it is one way of making the lesson easier for the pony. But as time goes on and the lesson has sunk in, if you repeat it only in that same place then the pony comes to think of it as something you do only there, and he won't do it anywhere else. Many people have been disappointed when they have trained a pony to behave beautifully in a school at home, and have gone to show someone else only to find that the pony does not appear to remember his lesson at all. Ponies, as we have seen, have a sharp memory for places: they know that certain front doors bring apples, or that the yard is where they get their feet picked up, or that the school is where they do their dressage patterns. To stop them doing this, as soon as they seem to have got the idea, on your fourth or fifth lesson, take them out of the place where they have learned it and repeat it somewhere else. After that, when you are polishing their learning, make half your lessons in the school and half in other places.

If you are to teach your pony well, then, you have to think about the times and places you choose, about how to make it easy for him to do the right thing, and about being calm yourself. Most of all, do as the Army maxim says: make much of your horse.

Chapter 10

Coping with obstinacy

We call a pony obstinate if he will not do what we ask, especially when we think he knows perfectly well what he should do. But there are several different reasons why he might refuse. He may be afraid; he may not understand; he may not be able to; he may not trust that particular rider; he may have got into the habit of refusing; or he may simply not like the idea. Deciding which can be difficult. Understanding the signals he is giving will help.

Fear

You can usually see when a pony is afraid, for she will be tense and alert. Her tail will usually be raised; she may dung; her eyes and ears will be directed at whatever scares her. But there are ponies that, instead of dancing about when they are afraid, freeze up like rabbits. The tension is still there in the mouth and neck, but the pony seems to be being pig-headed. My donkey, who is as 'obstinate' as they all are, refuses out of fear. The more you push her the more frightened she gets. She is frightened of quite silly things, like the shadows of trees forming stripes across the road on a bright day. A pony in this state does not need to be shouted at or beaten; she needs time to look at things properly, and she needs you to show her that there is no need to be afraid. As soon as she starts to move she should be praised warmly, for it will help get rid of the last of her fear.

Not understanding

A pony that does not understand does not show these signs of fear, unless you have flustered him by getting cross. Ponies often get upset when they are asked things they don't understand, and if you get worked up too they usually just try to leave, in rather a head-strong way. The pony does not need punishing, even for trying to escape; he needs bringing back to the problem calmly, facing it calmly, and being asked calmly and clearly what is wanted. When he realises he cannot escape he may still try to avoid the problem by switching off, standing like a statue and refusing to think about this impossible task. The more you try to force him the more switched off he will get; what you have to do is sit quietly until you feel his attention return, then ask again. Timing what you are asking so that he is most likely to take notice is important; you must also make sure that you are giving your signals clearly.

Impossibilities

Ponies sometimes cannot do what you ask. If you clutch the reins tight a pony will not go down a steep slope or a step, for she cannot see where she is going. If you stand in front of her, in the doorway of a stable, say, and pull her forwards she will refuse to come, for you appear to be asking her to step on top of you. She cannot know that you are planning to step aside. Ponies are sometimes too unfit or stiff to do what is asked: many stiff ponies find it difficult to bend to the right or lead on the off fore while cantering. There are exercises to make the pony more supple. If you practise these for a couple of weeks the pony's 'obstinacy' will miraculously disappear. A pony that is not feeling well, is tired or slightly lame may also appear to be obstinate. Do check that the pony can see and is well enough to do what you ask.

Habit

Ponies get into the habit of refusing if they are often allowed to do so. This is your problem, not theirs. Even the best-behaved pony can become stubborn if she is treated foolishly. Unfortunately beginners often do not have the self-confidence and determination to put their foot down when they need to. If nothing else seems to be wrong but the pony refuses to do something, you need to keep her head at it and keep pushing her. Usually that is all that is needed. The pony, seeing she is not going to be let off, eventually heaves a sigh and goes on, but she needs to be able to feel that you are saying 'Tough, that's where we're going' and meaning it. If, like not-so-effective riders, you think: 'Oh dear, perhaps I'd better try it this way' or 'She won't do it' or 'I don't want to push her, she might do something awful,' you will teach her to refuse. I have even heard people say 'Well, I'll try, but she won't do it, I know she won't.' Imagine what their body language is saying to that sensitive pony! Everything in you must be full of determination that you are going to succeed.

Dominic, Emma's older brother, was a bold, gentle, well-meaning fellow who had been ridden by village children who hadn't the faintest idea of how to ride and were in awe of his great strength. He marched cheerfully around the countryside with them doing exactly what he wanted. The first time I rode him I turned him round to close a gate and found he wouldn't go up to it. It took over two hours to get him to take two steps. He was astonished at the idea of being asked and made to do anything. But that one battle, a battle of wills rather than fisticuffs, fixed him: after that he was as good as gold with me, though he put everybody else to the test one by one, to see if they were the same kind of creature as me.

Determination

Many a beginner has said, 'My pony won't do that', only to be surprised and embarrassed when, with a different rider on board, the pony has not been her normal beastly self but has sailed through the difficulties willingly and easily. It is, of course, a question of riding skill as well as experience. But what the experienced person knows is that he *will* succeed. You learn that if you are even more obstinate than the pony, you will win. In fact, determined beginners can do just as well as more experienced people. It was not any riding skill that got Dominic up to that gate; it was my sheer refusal to let him do anything else. A beginner could have done that just as well. Dominic became a great beginner's horse, for his paces were easy and he soon taught every rider the value of being determined. You do not need to be rough, just determined.

If your pony has learned to be stubborn, don't give up. This means that sometimes you will be out well after dark, still pushing, still refusing to take no for an answer. It also means that you should think twice, especially if time is short, about what you ask the pony to do. Don't ask a difficult pony to do something he may refuse when you are in a hurry. Sure as fate he will pick up your feeling of not being wholly concentrated on the job, which weakens your determination, and you cannot afford to let him win just because you should be somewhere else.

Emma being obstinate about crossing a little ditch. She tried to turn away but Sian kept her head straight at it

She tried to turn the other way but Sian refused to let her escape. Sian was quite calm, not cross but determined, and pushing Emma on all the time

Emma then pulled the reins loose, not to get away, but . . .

. . . so that she could put her head down and have a good look, which she hadn't done before. Once she realised it was not so terrible she stepped over it quite calmly, just as the film ran out

Lack of trust

Some ponies refuse because they do not trust their riders. If you ride so badly that you hurt your pony's back and mouth every time you jump him, he will soon stop jumping for you even though he goes well for someone else. Pete is piggish about going into difficult places if he thinks his rider will lose her balance or grab at the reins. Timid and sensitive ponies tend to go along slowly and carefully if they don't think their riders are much good. If your pony refuses to canter with you but does so willingly for someone else, it is probably because he doesn't feel you're ready for it, even if you do. As you get less stiff and move better with the pony he will start to go more freely and willingly.

If you are worried about what is ahead your pony will feel that and is more likely to refuse, for a nervous rider always worries a pony. If you really don't think you can cope, remember that he is much more likely to follow you if you walk confidently ahead, and that getting through the problem in this way is better than having a disaster. Some people say that you should never get off, that it teaches the pony that he can get rid of you by kicking up a fuss; but it depends on the timing. As we have seen, timing is important in learning. If you let the pony scare you into getting off, he will indeed learn that it's a great trick. But if you dismount calmly before you get to the trouble he hasn't the faintest idea why. You may just have wanted to stretch your legs at that time (do tell yourself that, too). You may have wanted to check his shoes (do let him think that).

For instance, if you have to take a lorry-shy pony along a main road, don't ride along and throw yourself off when the first lorry appears: walk beside him the whole way. If you manage to get through the difficulties together, even with you on foot, it makes you both more confident in each other. Your pony will not know why you chose to walk that bit of road; what he will know is that you got him through it safely, and that there was a good feeling coming from you all the way. You can use this trust and build on it until he trusts you enough to let you ride him through without anybody being scared.

'I don't want to'

Ponies also have a shot at refusing to do things they don't feel like doing. They don't want to be caught; they don't want to leave their friends; they don't want to go that way. In the end it is sheer

Dolly comes ashore for the first time. The ramp is scarier than a trailer ramp because it keeps moving and making a grating noise on the shingle. Jane steps confidently forward, slightly to one side, making it clear to Dolly what she must do. I had my hand on Dolly's shoulder to calm her while the ramp was lowered, and left it there to keep her straight. We have made it easy for Dolly to be calm and relaxed.

Ponies are far less panicky in boats than in trailers when they first travel, for they are not shut in (Photo: Jane Turner)

persistence that wins. But you might also ask yourself why the idea is so hateful, and what you can do to make it better. Sometimes it is worth doing some deliberate reward training. I do not reward ponies much, but I do praise them, and when time is short rewards work quicker. Dolly, a young mare I borrowed as a packpony on a long journey, came from Bardsey Island where there are no cars, cows or trees. On her first day ashore I stopped every car that passed in the narrow lanes and explained her fear. Most were tourists happy to chat and offer her sandwiches, apples and toffee. By the second day she was quite keen on cars, and on the third day went through heavy traffic happily. But when she panicked at the sight of cows I heartlessly laughed, with the result that three months later she still loathed them. It was entirely my fault.

Chapter 11

Worse difficulties

If you have serious problems with your pony, it is up to you to do something about them, for the pony won't. If you go on doing whatever you are doing in the same way, even if that is what you have been taught is 'correct', the pony will go on responding in the same way. That doesn't mean the problems are your fault: they may be due to bad handling or bad experiences before you got him. But whichever side the fault lies on, don't sink into despair and guilt. Everybody who has had ponies has had problems at some time or another, and every time you solve them you learn something new. The great thing is to be positive that you can work out the reason and what to do to improve matters. For there will be a solution. Out of the many 'problem' horses I've worked with there hasn't been one that didn't improve enormously with different handling, even when they had to be kept in ways that neither they nor I liked.

One dreadful horse was a stallion in a racing yard which, when I first worked there, had become short of staff. Only after several days of hectic work did I discover him, tucked in a dark box round a corner, filthy, knee-deep in dung, and obviously unexercised. I couldn't understand why he should be so neglected: he was a beautiful and valuable racehorse. The lads said, 'You can clean him out then,' pushed me into his box with a broom and shovel, and locked me in. Instantly the horse attacked, screaming, flailing at me with his front feet as he lunged open-mouthed at me. Serious stuff: he was out to kill. Almost without thinking I rammed the broom-handle into his mouth. Immediately he dropped to the ground again and stood, surprised, sucking the broom-handle like a baby with a dummy. I mucked out round him until they came to release me.

In the week that followed I gradually cleaned out the stable and polished the horse, but to pay back the lads I always shut the top door so they couldn't see how I was doing it. They never cottoned on to why I needed two brooms. The stallion never stopped going for me, but his attacks weren't serious any more: he was reaching for his broom-handle, not for me.

That was a genuinely crazed horse, and I was lucky in hitting on that crazy solution. It wasn't the best way, which would have been to turn out the horse, but it worked: I had a safe way of handling him, I could groom him (he almost purred when I did) and, most important, I could give him the company and comfort he so desperately needed.

Whatever your problems with your pony, they can't be as bad as that. And if that had a solution, so will your problems. Take heart.

Working out why you have a problem

Ponies have different reasons for doing the same thing. For instance, they may run away because they are frightened, because they are too full of energy, because they love racing, because they have been taught to race, because the bit is too hard, because the bit is too soft, or because you don't ride well enough to stop them. Obviously, your solution depends on why they are doing it.

The first step is to decide whether it is you or the pony that needs retraining. The quickest way to find out is to ask someone experienced to ride or handle the pony, explaining what the difficulty is. Although approaching someone you may not know well will take courage on your part, it is unlikely you will be refused if you ask politely. You are asking only ten minutes of their time.

During that ten minutes, forget your own feelings and watch carefully. Watch your expert's body language as much as what he does; watch your pony's response. You can learn an incredible amount in ten minutes. You will soon see if it is your riding that is at fault. If not, your expert may have suggestions about your tack, feeding, or have other ideas.

Another pointer to the cause of the trouble is whether the pony has got better, worse, or stayed the same since you got him. If he's got better, you're clearly on the right track. Be patient, and remember that it takes a pony weeks or months to drop a bad habit even when the cause for it has disappeared. If he's got worse, you're clearly doing something that doesn't suit him. If he's stayed the same, he has a habit that you haven't yet found how to deal with.

Heavy hands make misery and problems. This pony, and thousands like her all over Britain, is having a horrible time, as you can see from her face, ears and tail. Her rider thinks that 'contact' means a firm pull on the reins, which the pony hates. Although his position looks good, the rider is so stiff and tense that he is pulling himself out of the saddle, feels unsafe, and balances by hanging on the pony's mouth. He should balance on his bottom, not his hands, try to loosen up, and give the pony a much lighter rein. This is a quiet, kind pony that puts up with her misery. Other don't. They run away, rear, get nervous or obstinate, refuse to be caught or try to escape in other ways.

Always ride with the lightest possible touch; always try to improve your hands; and if you have problems, always suspect your hands are causing them

Finding further help

There are people who specialise in working with problem horses. The best way to find them is through your vet, blacksmith, local Pony Club or riding club (even if you aren't a member).

If your riding needs improving, try joining the Pony Club or going for a private lesson at a riding school with your pony. You will learn far more in a half-hour private lesson than in hours in a class. But instructors vary enormously; good ones are wonderful and bad ones useless, so again ask around to find out who is recommended. Do not be afraid to ask questions; there are reasons for everything you do in riding, and you are more likely to remember what to do if you understand why it works. Unlike other pupils, you can go home and practise what you've learned.

Working on your own

To work out what is troubling the pony you need to be sensitive to his body language. Certainly he is telling you what is the matter. Could it be that you are deaf?

Secondly, get thinking about your own body language, your carelessness and your bad riding habits. We all have them. Some ponies put up with them; others don't.

Thirdly, consider how ponies would like to live, whether your pony's lifestyle comes near that, and what you could do to make it better.

Finally, be kind. Even when the pony is beastly to you, even when you have to be firm with him, be kind. Ponies aren't old boots, to be kicked around and thrown in corners. Even the beastliest of them improves with kindness. Put yourself in his place. Be kind.

Disaster areas: possible causes of problems

Causes	Troubles	What to do
Mistakes in handling:		
standing in wrong place (wrong body chess)	pony difficult to handle, groom, catch, lead, clean feet	think and experiment; on the whole, stay close, keeping one hand on pony, so he doesn't feel you're stabbing at him
holding too tight: pony can't see	'obstinacy' or panic	loosen up; remember about ponies' eyes
Bad timing:		
a) pony not experienced enough for what you're asking	refusal e.g. to jump; panic; pony gets rattled	train in gradual steps; see Ch. 9
b) pony not paying attention: too much going on, or too frisky	pony ignores you	settle with steady trotting or simple work until he attends; watch his ears; see Ch. 5

Continued on page 158

Causes	Troubles	What to do
c) badly timed punishment	pony doesn't learn; gets angry, vicious or sullen	see Ch. 9
d) badly timed approach	pony won't be caught	see 'hard to catch' p.167
You are nervous	so is the pony; or he doesn't want you near him	see Ch. 6
You are rushed	pony gets rattled	see Ch. 6
You dither	pony does what he wants, or stops listening	see Ch. 6
You are not nice to him	pony won't be caught; nappy (tries to go home)	appreciate him
Bad riding:		
bad hands: too rough, too jerky	running away; rearing; napping; jibbing (stopping suddenly); pony nervous, won't go forward boldly	the commonest cause of difficulty; see (**1**) below
too much 'contact'	stiffens neck and sticks out head; pony feels heavy; hard mouth; head-tossing	loosen up; make your arms and hands elastic, not stiff; don't lean forward
Bad seat:		
a) not using seat to stop	pony won't stop	see (**1**) below
b) bad balance	pony won't go fast, jump, or go into difficult places; you fall off!	bad balance upsets the pony's balance and scares him; do exercises
c) leaning forward	excitable pony gets more excitable; sluggish pony gets more sluggish; hard to turn; won't stop	see (**1**) below
not using aids well (not using legs)	pony won't turn	see (**1**) below
you don't think ahead	pony 'gets away' with things	see (**2**) below

Causes	Troubles	What to do
Management doesn't suit the pony:		
overfeeding	pony excitable, runs aways, bucks, frisky	see Ch.7
underfeeding	pony sluggish and tired	see Ch. 7
cold	pony grumpy	
too cooped up	pony excitable, fretful, bad-tempered; weaving, crib-biting, wind-sucking, rug-chewing, banging and kicking in box, etc.	see Ch. 5 for signs. Arrange more freedom or company in box; build pen outside stable so pony can go out
lonely	pony silly in company, miserable	arrange company. See **(3)** below
Tack doesn't suit:		
bit too harsh	pony nervous, head-tosses, afraid to go forward	experiment by sewing layers of material over your bit; borrow rubber or vulcanite bit
bit too soft	pony won't stop	less likely than bad seat or other causes; see **(4)** below
doesn't like a bit	pony nervous, goes with hollow back, star-gazes, head-tosses	common in Arabs. Try a gentle hackamore but take advice on fitting and handling, and school in it before hacking out
saddle doesn't fit	pony bucks; kicks when girth done up; sore back, leading to rearing and refusal to jump	feel pony's back for hot spots. Put saddle on without a numnah and make sure it doesn't touch pony's spine with someone on it (you should see light looking from back to front)
Trouble on pony's side:		
bad habit	e.g. leaps forward as you mount, knocks you over, etc.	see **(5)** below
pony afraid	nervous, nappy, won't go forward	gain his trust by being with him, taking him for walks; ride with others
pony too strong for you	barges off when led; runs away	see **(6)** below
something wrong physically	see Ch. 10; bad backs cause bucking; odd going downhill or cantering	feel and watch carefully; vet.

Lady, a sensitive little Arab, has a very soft mouth, and although Ceri is gentle with her hands Lady sticks her nose in the air and hollows her back. Because she was afraid of the bit Lady kept running away, and Ceri was unable to stop her without hurting her, which made the problem worse

1 This book is not about how to ride, but if you don't understand the basic principles of riding you are bound to have problems. Unfortunately most people are taught many details without ever learning these basic ideas. If you are a beginner you will need to learn the details as well: consult a book on learning to ride.

a) Riding is about getting from A to B. The pony must go forward freely.
b) A pony's engine is his hindquarters: his power comes from behind you.
c) The aids (legs, seat, weight, hands) put pressure on different parts of the pony, and he moves to make himself more comfortable by taking the pressure off.
d) The pony is like a see-saw, with you sitting in the middle.

When a pony is afraid of your hurting his mouth, or if you are unbalancing him by sitting badly, he doesn't go forward freely and joyfully; he tries to escape the misery. The way he chooses depends

When we borrowed a hackamore for her (it's too big and comes too far down her nose) Lady was instantly much happier. This problem is common with Arabs. If you ride with a soft bit and loose rein, or no bit, they stop fighting, panicking and bolting.

Ceri's stirrups are too short so that she sits too far back in the saddle, which again tends to make Lady hollow her back

on his character. He may get over-excited, rearing or trying to turn back because his fear builds an invisible wall in front of him; he may try to get rid of you; or he may stiffen his mouth and neck so he seems insensitive. Be gentle with the reins: squeeze them, don't yank on them.

When a pony uses his back-end power to go faster, either because he wants to or because you've asked him, he drops his hindquarters and coils his back legs under him, the better to leap forwards. If you then take a hold on the reins, that energy pushing from behind is stopped from in front, so he becomes like a coiled spring. However, if you take a hold without that energy pushing from behind, all you do is put a dead weight on the rein, which he resents. When out hacking, have your reins short enough for you to stop but let your arms and hands be completely free and elastic. If you want his energy bottled up, so he is springier and livelier to ride, ask him to make more power with his back end. When he starts to go faster, control his speed by taking a hold.

As aids to turning, your legs are more important than your hands, and again you should always use them before your hands. Push the pony's hindquarters in the direction you want by squeezing your heel against his opposite side; then move both hands slightly towards the way you want to go and squeeze the rein on that side. Pulling on one rein, a common beginner's fault, only makes a pony bend his head towards the pull: it doesn't ask him to turn his shoulders or hindquarters at all. To turn his shoulder, move your outside rein (the one opposite to the way you want to go) towards his neck so it pushes against his neck and shoulder. If he's difficult to turn, and won't even turn his head in the right direction when you use the rein on that side, remember to use this outside rein to push his shoulder over. You'll find it works better if you raise your outside hand slightly, for then he bends his neck down and towards your inside rein.

By pushing forward with your seat you push the pony forwards.

When you are approaching any difficulty, like going down a steep hill, stay calm and trust your pony. If you are nervous, like this rider, you tense up, stiffening your legs so that you push yourself out of the saddle. Clutching at the reins stops the pony from being able to see, so he too gets frightened. This pony will either refuse to go on or, if he is a nervous type, may panic and do something stupid. This rider is in real danger because the only thing keeping her on is her tight leg, which is exciting the pony; and she has little control with the reins because the pony's neck is so tense

As soon as you sit down in the saddle and relax your leg you feel safer and the pony calms down. Leaving your rein loose allows him to stretch his neck and pick his footing as he walks on quietly.

Many people in Britain ride with far too short a stirrup. Although it feels safer it isn't, for you tend to rise from the saddle and tense your legs, driving the pony faster. The only way you can stop then is to pull the reins, which hurts and upsets the pony. Learn to ride with your stirrups long and improve your balance; learn to calm the pony by sitting well down and relaxing your leg; and most of all, learn to ride with a lighter hand and looser rein. You will find you have more control, not less, for the pony will not be fighting you

By pressing down with it you slow him down. By standing up you let him coil his back legs under himself and spring forwards.

When you lean sideways, especially when going fast (watch polo players), the pony moves sideways to put himself underneath you again. When you lean back you slow him down. Using your weight like this isn't considered elegant, but it works. Leaning back and pressing down with your seat is the only way you'll stop a real runaway. You should also try to break the rhythm of his gallop by giving short pulls on the reins: if you pull steadily he can use that to coil himself up against. Throwing him from one side to the other, or forcing him to turn sharply, also helps to stop a pony that is trying to use your pull on the reins to help him spring forwards more powerfully.

When a pony is going along slowly, without his energy all bottled up, if you lean forward you tip his see-saw down in front and drive his front end down into the ground. This makes him feel sluggish, heavy and difficult to turn. Make sure you are sitting up straight, tall and free. If you then push forwards with your seat you'll make the pony drop his back end and raise his front: you'll see his head rise. He'll respond to the aids better, too.

Take your pony to a quiet, enclosed place (not his own field, for that is full of special spots as far as he's concerned) and experiment with these ideas while he is quiet and relaxed. Try using just your legs; try using your hands differently; try with just your seat or your weight, before starting to put them together. You will certainly find that your pony responds to some aids better than others. This depends a lot on how he has been ridden before. No two ponies are the same, and if you're having difficulty controlling him you probably haven't hit on quite the right balance of aids for him yet. Remember, though: legs before hands, and be gentle with your hands.

2 Good riders think ahead of their horses. When Max passes a certain mare's field she rushes to the fence. If I just sat and expected him to go past he'd suddenly rear and end up half-way over the fence. Instead, I start telling him we're going to trot past long before we get to the field, and we do (rather bouncily and noisily).

When you know you're going to have a disagreement with your pony – for instance, she always wants to turn left at some particular turning – start telling her what you're going to do before she starts doing the opposite. It's easier to make up her mind for her before any trouble starts than to change it once she's thought of her wicked idea.

3 If you can't keep her with another pony, consider a donkey. But remember that donkeys are desert animals: their coats are not waterproof and they must have shelter in the winter. A pony and a donkey will happily share the same stable.

4 You can use a Pelham to retrain a pony that keeps running away, but first you will have to learn to use double reins properly. You must be able to use the snaffle rein without the curb, and put pressure on the curb only when you want. Practise this while riding quietly, without the pony ever getting a chance to run away. When you have mastered it, take him out and let him gallop. The idea is that you give the pony the chance to stop on the snaffle rein. If he doesn't (he won't, at first), you stop him with the curb. As you ask him to stop with the snaffle rein alone, say 'whoa'. If he doesn't

When you are working round a pony, putting the bridle on, grooming him or picking out his feet, stay close, with your body touching his, so that he can feel where you are. Otherwise he is likely to move away to try to see you

slow down within a few strides, stop him firmly with the curb. Your timing must be good, and you must use praise and reward, for you are teaching him. It will take time, but he will learn. You may find that after a few months back on a snaffle bit he needs another retraining session; or you may find that you end up riding him in a Pelham without the curb rein.

5 If you are sure there is nothing else wrong, and if the pony has always had the habit, first of all try to arrange things so that the pony can't repeat his beastliness. For instance, mount facing a corner, have someone hold him, or even tie him up while you get on. (I once knew an old cowboy who for twenty-three years of daily riding always had to tie up his mule when he got on. As he was an excellent trainer I asked if it wasn't possible to teach her to stand still, but he simply said 'Ain't no sense in argifyin' with a mule!') Praise and reward him when he behaves, even when you've given him no chance to do wrong. When a pony can't repeat his habit he eventually drops it, but it can take months.

After this first period of avoiding the danger area, think carefully about how you can break it down into separate parts so you can retrain him properly.

If you have a pony that has a revolting trick like dropping one shoulder and swerving in mid-gallop, or scraping you against trees, you will simply have to learn to read the warning signs quicker and think ahead of him more. Again you will find if he can't repeat the habit, he will drop it.

6 Sometimes you get a pony that realises you're not as strong and competent as his previous owner, and starts taking advantage of you. There are ways of making a halter more forceful: by running the lead rope from the side ring on the opposite side, over his nose, and through the ring on your side; or, stronger still, by running it from the ring on your side, over his poll, through the ring on the opposite side, and then over his nose; best of all, by using a specially designed 'be nice' halter which tightens up when the pony pulls, but slackens immediately he behaves.

Lead him with a whip in your left hand, bringing it up level with his nose when he starts pulling, so he feels blocked. You can do this even with your hand.

School the pony in enclosed spaces until you have worked out how to control him. *Don't* be tempted to get rough and 'teach the horse who's master'; you will end up in a real mess. You have to win him over: the more you can make a friend of him the safer you'll be.

A 'be nice' halter, useful for badly behaved ponies that tow you away when you are leading them. The halter is made of thin cord that tightens when the pony pulls, but loosens as soon as he behaves himself. Do not pull on the halter yourself, but leave the lead rope slack. The pony soon learns that he hurts himself by behaving riotously, and that he is comfortable when he walks quietly. If you pull or jerk at the halter the lesson isn't so clear.

You can make one of these yourself using nylon cord and rings from a sailing or climbing shop. The noseband cord is knotted on the side rings. The throatlatch cords run freely through the side rings and the back ring, where they cross over. You might want to put a toggle on the cord round the back of the chin to tighten it after putting it on, or the pony could wriggle out of the halter by jumping backwards and ducking his head

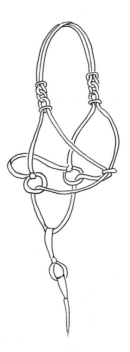

Hard to catch. Even if your pony is easy to catch, always take a titbit or a bucket. It is easy and natural for a pony to avoid being caught, so make sure she is rewarded. Show the reward, not the work: hold out the bucket, not the rope. Many ponies have at first been caught by being cornered, and their natural feelings have been strengthened. The only way to break them down is to keep the pony in a small space and catch her ten or twenty times daily with a bucket, so that she feeds mainly from your hand. When you return her to the field, get her to come to you, or rather the bucket, as many times as you have time for, not just when you want to use her.

If you chase, corner, or try to pounce on a pony you turn yourself into an attacker and him into a wild animal. If you do have to corner your pony, give him time to relax before moving in on him. If he turns his bottom on you and you know he is likely to kick, wallop the ground behind his heels hard with a whirling rope, so he jumps forward and turns to face you. Praise him immediately: facing you is half the problem.

A pony that is hard to catch only on good spring grass can be taught to tether, but be sure to use a chain or very fat rope at first, or he will rope-burn himself.

Once you have set out to catch a pony, don't give up.

Problems without solutions

There are, unfortunately, a few.

1 The horse has a brain tumour. This is sometimes suggested as the cause of a horse behaving riotously for no apparent reason. However, brain tumours are extremely rare. I have met several horses that were thought to have brain tumours, but none of them did; they were either afraid, suffering from back pain or muscle damage, or someone had not thought deeply enough about the cause of their behaviour.

2 The horse is simply a rogue. Frankly, I don't believe it; but it may take someone who is experienced in dealing with difficult horses to sort him out. No horse is born bad; they are made bad, and what's made can be unmade.

3 You and the pony aren't suited. Sadly, this is possible. When you buy a pony you must be realistic about what you want the pony to do and how you are going to keep him. It is also important to have the opinion of someone really experienced with lots of different types of ponies, for he will be a quicker judge of a pony's character than you. Sometimes a pony of rather the opposite character to you will bring out a side of you that you barely knew existed; but sometimes he will depress and frighten you. For instance, a gentle, timid person would not be well suited to a strong, bold, lively cob, though a jolly extrovert would love him.

If you are disappointed that you don't seem to 'click' with your pony, don't despair straight away. Remember that ponies do change and learn. Try retraining him and yourself, and give it your best shot. But if after six months you still feel it's hopeless, you may both be better parting company. This is especially true if the pony frightens you.

Chapter 12

Ends and beginnings

The men did poorly on the round-up. The horses were too wary, too well led: the old white mare seemed to have eyes in the back of her clever head. Only one colt, driven away by the stallion, was taken. He stands pitifully alone, cringing and starting, in the pen, still shaking from the horror of the strange-smelling animals and their strange-smelling horses, the hissing of the ropes and the clash of the gates. All night he trembles and listens, quivering in his terrible, naked loneliness.

In the morning the boy brings water and sweet grass, lies down and reads a book. For two hours the colt stands rigid in the opposite corner, hardly daring to peek at the strange long body lying motionless on the grass. Only long after the boy has gone does he creep hesitantly over to the grass and snatch a mouthful, catching that strange-animal smell on it as he scuttles back to his corner. Another mouthful, another retreat. A third, and the boy comes back, scaring him rigid again. But the colt is ravenously hungry, and after only an hour he reaches forward to lip the fallen strands of grass nearest him, keeping a wary eye on the boy and backing away hastily each time he grabs a bit. But the boy does not move, nor even look; he is as unconcerned as a grazing rabbit.

When the colt has finished the pieces he dropped there is only the great heap of grass that the boy is sprawling on. The colt looks with one eye, then the other. He wants it. But he cannot tell what the boy will do. He stamps experimentally. The boy takes no notice. He shakes his head a little. Still no reaction. The colt yawns, flicks his tail, and scratches his side, but these do not interest the boy either. He seems busy at whatever he's doing. Finally the colt sighs and walks slowly round to the grass at the boy's feet. It takes a

great deal of courage to reach for a mouthful, but he does it. And the boy still takes no notice, even when he scuffles backwards and drops half his grass.

This is a very strange animal. It is frightening, but it does not attack. It has no fear: it does not run away. It makes a lot of strange noises, some deep, some high, some twittering, like birds. It can stand high like an angry bear or squirm like a snake. It can clasp things in its paws like a squirrel. It has no ears, and it makes its bed of the best grass . . .

Backwards and forwards goes the colt, watching and thinking as he steals the bed, twenty times, thirty times. He has been so close that the smell of the boy's bare feet has filled his nostrils. Now he reaches for another mouthful and drifts his nose over the heel and ankle before he steps back to watch. He knows the boy must have felt him, but there is still no reaction. There is something covering the boy's leg, and next time he advances he tries to lift it off with his teeth. But the leg comes too, terrifying him so he cannot let go but leaps backwards until the cloth rips from his teeth. He stands snorting in his corner. But the boy only moves lazily, nickering softly in his strange way, before settling down. The colt will not try that again. But it is hard to know what to do, without the guidance of the others.

At nightfall the boy leaves for long enough for the colt to follow the smell of water and drink thirstily. But the bucket, too, is strange, and in pulling back from it he tips it over. When the boy returns with his blanket he fetches more, but the colt will not drink while he holds it.

The boy sleeps so soundly that the colt works round him steadily, letting his nose brush the boy's body each time he steals a mouthful. Even when he is bold enough to try pushing under the legs for grass he still backs away a couple of steps so he can see while he munches, but he no longer has to retreat to his corner until he wishes for sleep. He dozes on his feet, aware of the still, calm, alien presence. When the dogs bark, startling him, the boy merely stirs, raises his head and calls softly to him and the colt, peering at him through the gloom, sees he is still unafraid and is strangely comforted.

Hot, sweet breath on his face wakes the boy. Soft whiskered lips trickle over his, feeling, testing, tasting. For both of them this moment of contact is shocking, full of feeling: on the colt's part, of fear and curiosity, loneliness and longing; on the boy's, of delight and dreams, desire and relief. For his patience, tact and understanding have paid off, and this wild creature has freely chosen to come to him. Now the colt takes a step back in a different way, easily, quietly, as if he has completed some project and can relax at last. Side by side they doze again in the thin light of dawn.

By the end of the day the colt has touched the boy three times, mussed his hair, and is no longer panic-stricken when he moves. He has drunk again, allowing the boy to hold his bucket. In the evening, when the boy disappears for a couple of hours, the colt feels the weight of loneliness again. When the boy returns with another bundle of grass, the colt takes a step towards him. The boy comes forward slowly, watching carefully, until he gauges that the colt will allow him no nearer. Then he backs slowly away to his side of the pen. Again the colt steps forward, almost as if he cannot help himself.

This is the beginning: one step forward, a hesitant bridging of the gap between them. Yet this gulf will be filled by the bonds that both of them know; the need for closeness, for company, for trust, cemented by their growing understanding of each other's ways. There will be mutual pleasures: the first time the colt feels fingers on him and forgets his fear in the joy of having the dried mud and sweat rubbed and loosened; his slow following of the boy around the pen; the sweetness of a shared apple. There will be irritation, when the colt is hungry and does not want to be bothered by hands on him before he eats, or when the boy is impatient at his slow progress. There will be fear, when the colt first feels the rope around his neck, only to realise it is no more than a physical sign of the bond that is already between them, or when the boy first opens the gate of the pen to lead him out, knowing that if he has mistaken the moment and the bond is not strong enough he will lose his colt, rope or no rope. There will be work: hours, days, months, years of it, until you would see them as no different from any other rider on a well-trained horse, and would never guess that this one slow step had been the beginning. And throughout it all they will watch each other, and think, and learn.

There is no end. You can spend a lifetime watching and thinking and learning, wherever you start. That is where understanding comes from. Books can teach you only things, bits of knowledge; but knowledge isn't understanding. If you don't use your eyes and your brain, no person or book or pony can help you, for understanding can grow only from using your awareness.

Go to it.

Index

accidents, 85, 102, 140
aids, 96–7
alarm calls, 91
Arabs, 78, 109, 112
attack, body language,
  80–1

barging, 86–7
bellies, sensitive places, 80
biting, 80–1
  bad habits, 82
  punishment for, 141–2
  rider's feet, 78–9
  warning signs, 74, 80
bits:
  head-tossing, 78
  taking bridles off, 70–2
Black Jack, 80, 140
body language:
  body chess, 86–8
  cooped up ponies, 82–4
  defence and attack, 80–1
  ears, 68–9
  eyes, 70
  face, 70–4
  movements, 76–80
  pony's, 53–88, 94, 157
  rider's, 97–106, 157
  shape of the body, 55–68
  sweats and shivers, 84–5
  tails, 74–6
bolting, 25
boredom, 72, 91
brain tumours, 168
brains, 7–8
breaking-in ponies, 78,
  169–72

bridles:
  Pelham, 164–6
  taking off, 70–2
brumbies, 21
bullies, 121–6

calls, 88–92
catching ponies, 167
character, 107–20
charging, 80
Clever Hans, 106
Cobs, 50, 110, 112
colic, 64, 72, 74
colour vision, 43
colts:
  games, 30
  gelding, 118
commands, voice, 95–6
concentrates, 118
cooped up ponies, 82–4
cows, fear of, 29
crib-biting, 82
cringing, 66–8
curiosity, body
  language, 60

day and night, 22–3
deer, 46–7
defence, body language,
  80–1
determination, 149
diarrhoea, 76
Dink, 122–4
Dolly, 50, 153
Dominic, 149
donkeys, 29, 84, 124, 164

dressage, 76
dullness, body language,
  62–6
dung, smelling, 45–6
dunging, 76, 81, 92

ears:
  body language, 68–9
  flattened, 80
  hearing, 43–4
  sick ponies, 64
earthquakes, 51
Emma, 72, 122–5
excitement, body
  language, 55–6
experience, 114–15
eyes:
  body language, 70
  colour vision, 43
  eyesight, 35–43, 157, 162
  field of vision, 36–40
  focusing, 40–1
  night sight, 42–3
  seeing movement, 41–2
  sick ponies, 64

face, body language, 70–4
family ties, 127
fear, 23–4, 147
  body language, 56–9,
  66–8, 69
  rider's 99–101
  signs of, 84
  teaching a pony not to
    be afraid, 134–41
feather, 79–80

feet (pony's):
  care of, 29–30
  kicking, 80
  pawing, 79
  picking up, 101, 136
  stamping, 79–80
  warning signs, 79
feet (rider's), biting, 78–9
field of vision, 36–40
fighting, 81, 90
flattened ears, 69
flehmen, 44, 72
flies:
  head-shaking, 78
  horseflies, 79
  kicking at, 80
  skin-wriggling, 85
  stamping, 79
  tail-lashing, 76
foals:
  body language, 86
  mouthing, 74
  orphans, 127
focusing, eyes, 40–1
food:
  and pony's character, 118, 120
  taste, 47–8
Fred, 137–40
French National Equestrian Centre, 142–3
friends, 31, 34, 84, 88, 122–5, 129–32
frightened ponies see fear
fun, body language, 59–60

games, 30–1, 86–8, 104–6
Gandhi, 29–30
geldings, 118
goats, 84
groans, 91
grooming, 50, 72
grumpiness, 66
grunts, 91

habits, 82–4
halters, 166
handling ponies, 112–14
Hawk, 123–5
head-jerks, 76
head movements, body language, 76–9
head-shaking, 82
head-thrusts, 78, 80, 82
hearing, 43–4
high blowing, 92

hormones, 118–20
horseflies, 79
hunters and hunted, 23–4, 35–6

inheritance, 109–10

Jacobson's organ, 44
jawing, 74
jumping, 30

kicking, 70, 80, 141–2

laminitis, 64
language:
  aids, 96–7
  pony's voice, 88–92
  rider's voice, 95–6
  smells, 92
  see also body language
lashing tails, 76, 80
leaders, 121, 124–5, 126–7
learning, 8, 133–46
leg movements, body language, 79–80
lips, body language, 72, 74
loneliness, 32

Maestoso, 89, 104, 107–8, 126, 129
Mangas, 32, 70, 86, 114, 122–4, 130–2
maps, mental, 27
mares:
  body language, 79, 86, 87
  calls, 90
  fighting, 81
  leaders, 121, 124–5
  mating, 75, 92
  in season, 75, 90, 92, 120
massage, 50–1
mating, 75, 92, 120
Max, 48, 50, 84, 85, 89–90, 92, 107–8, 109, 119–20, 164
medicines, 48
meeting other ponies, 62
memory, 13–14, 17, 26–7
Moifaa, 21
moods, 117–18
Moonie, 29, 52
mouth:

body language, 70–2
  fear, 57
  relaxation, 62–4
  mouthing, 74
movement:
  body language, 62, 76–80
  seeing, 41–2
Muffin, 115–17
mustangs, 21

neck, stiffness, 57–8
neck-wringing, 78
neighing, 88–90
nickering, 90
night and day, 22–3
night sight, 42–3
nipping, 81
noses:
  body language, 72
  nose-blowing, 91–2
  sense of smell, 44–7
  sense of touch, 50
  whiskers, 48–9
nostrils, body language, 72, 74
nudging, 76–8

obstinacy, 147–53
older ponies, 115–17
outlines, body language, 68

pain:
  body language, 72, 74
  groans, 91
  signs of, 84
paths, 28
pawing, 79
pee, smell-messages, 92
Pelham bridles, 164–6
Pete, 10–14, 25, 26–7, 41–2, 46–7, 50, 62, 72–4, 76–8, 89–90, 91, 99–100, 107, 109, 119–20, 122–4, 130–2, 133, 140
pigs, fear of, 29, 68, 91
plants, poisonous, 48
play, 30–1, 59–60, 86–8, 104–6, 141
poisonous plants, 48
polo ponies, 86
Pony Club, 143–4, 156
pony-talk, 54–5
praise, 114–15, 136–7, 144, 153

problems, 154–68
punishments, 141–3

reins, 39–40
relaxation, 51, 57, 62–4,
    70–2, 91, 100, 134–6,
    145
remembering, 13–14, 17,
    26–7
resting places, 25–6
rewards, 153
riders:
    aids, 96–7
    body language, 97–106
    voice, 95–6
riding schools, 156–7
rigs, 118–19
roaring, 92
roars, 90
Rogers, Roy, 134
rolling, 79
rolling eyes, 70
running away, 24–5, 97,
    155, 163, 164–6

saddles, sore backs, 85
Sam, 32
sand-colic, 66
scratching, 45, 50, 72
screams, 90
season, mares, 75, 90, 92,
    120
senses, 35–52
    eyes, 35–43
    hearing, 43–4
    shaking, 51–2
    size, 52
    smells, 44–7
    taste, 47–8
    touch, 49–51
    whiskers, 48–9
Shakertown, 94
shaking, 51–2
sheep, 84
shelters, 25–6
shivering, 84–5
shock, 85

shoulder-barging, 86–7
shying, 39
sick ponies, 64–6, 69, 91
sighs, 91
size, 52
skin-wriggling, 85
sleep, 32
smell, sense of, 27
smells, language of, 44–7,
    92
snakes, fear of, 28–9, 74,
    81
snorts, 91
Soda, 114
Sophie, 122–5
spooking, 22
squeals, 90
stable vices, 82–4
stables, 26, 82–4
'stallion smile', 44
stallions:
    body language, 55
    calls, 88, 90, 91
    fighting, 81
    Flehmen, 44, 72
    games, 30
    hormones, 118–20
    mating, 75, 92
    neck-wringing, 78
    wild, 15–16
stamping, 79–80
startled ponies, 58
steeplechasing, 30
sweating, 84

tail-lashing, 76, 80
tails, body language, 62,
    74–6
'talk', 54–5
taste, 47–8
teeth:
    biting, 74, 78–9, 80–1,
        82, 141–2
    warning signs, 70, 74, 80
    yawning, 72
tension, 57–9, 70–2, 91
Tess, 122–5
testosterone, 118–20

Thoroughbreds, 50, 109,
    112
ticklish ponies, 50
tigers, fear of, 23–4, 28
tiredness, 72
titbits, 76, 132
torches, 42–3
tossing heads, 78
touch, 49–51
tracking, 46–7
treacle, 48
trekking ponies, 28
trembling, 84–5
Trigger, 133–4
trust, lack of, 152
Tschiffely, 34

Van Osten, 106
vocal cords, whistling and
    roaring, 92
voice:
    pony's, 88–92
    rider's, 44, 95–6

warning signs:
    of attack, 80
    before kicking, 80
    ears, 69
    leg movements, 79
    teeth, 70, 74, 80
water, fear of, 137–40
weaving, 82
whinnying, 88–90
whiskers, 48–9
whisking tails, 76
whistling, 92
wild horses, 15–20, 21–2,
    169–72
wind-sucking, 82
word commands, 44
wormer nuts, 48
wrinkling noses, 72

yawning, 72
yearlings, mouthing, 74